Writing
about
Music

THIRD
EDITION

Writing
about
Music

AN INTRODUCTORY GUIDE

Richard J. Wingell

University of Southern California

Prentice
Hall

Upper Saddle River, New Jersey 07458

Library of Congress Cataloging-in-Publication Data

WINGELL, RICHARD
  Writing about music : an introductory guide / Richard J. Wingell—3rd ed.
    p. cm.
  Includes index.
  ISBN 0-13-040603-1
  1. Music—Historiography—Handbooks, manuals, etc. 2. Musical
  criticism—Authorship—Handbooks, manuals, etc. 3. Academic writing—Handbooks,
  Manuals, etc. I. Title.

  ML3797.W54 2002
  808'.06678—dc21   2001045945

Senior acquisitions editor: *Christopher T. Johnson*
Editorial assistant: *Evette Dickerson*
Project manager: *Carole R. Crouse*
Prepress and manufacturing buyer: *Benjamin Smith*
Copy editor: *Carole R. Crouse*
Marketing manager: *Chris Ruel*
Cover designer: *Bruce Kenselaar*

This book was set in 9.5/12 Stone Serif by ElectraGraphics, Inc.,

The cover was printed by Phoenix Color Corp.

Examples 1 and 2 (pages 162 and 163): © Copyright 1908, 1909 by Adolf Furstner. U.S. Copyright
Renewed. Copyright Assigned 1943 to Hawkes & Son (London) Ltd., a Boosey & Hawkes company
for the world excluding Germany, Italy, Portugal and the Former Territories of the U.S.S.R.
(excluding Estonia, Latvia, and Lithuania).

© 2002, 1997, 1990 by Pearson Education, Inc.
Upper Saddle River, New Jersey 07458

Printed in the United States of America

10 9 8

ISBN: 0-13-040603-1

PEARSON EDUCATION LTD., *London*
PEARSON EDUCATION AUSTRALIA PTY, LIMITED, *Sydney*
PEARSON EDUCATION SINGAPORE, PTE. LTD.
PEARSON EDUCATION NORTH ASIA LTD., *Hong Kong*
PEARSON EDUCATION CANADA, LTD., *Toronto*
PEARSON EDUCACIÓN DE MEXICO, S.A., DE C.V.
PEARSON EDUCATION--JAPAN, *Tokyo*
PEARSON EDUCATION MALAYSIA, PTE. LTD.
PEARSON EDUCATION, *Upper Saddle River, New Jersey*

Contents

Preface   xi

1   Writing about Music   1
Why We Write about Music, 1
The Special Challenges of Writing about Music, 2
Inappropriate Ways to Write about Music, 3
Musicological Research and Writing, 7

2   Analysis and Research   9
Analysis, 9
Questions to Consider, 10
Examples of Works and Research Directions, 13
   Gesualdo: "Moro, lasso," *13*
   J. S. Bach: Opening Chorus of Cantata No. 80, Ein' feste Burg ist unser Gott, *14*
   Mozart: Concerto for Piano and Orchestra in C Minor, K. 491, First Movement, 16
   Verdi: Otello, *Act I, Scene 3, 17*
   Liszt: A Faust Symphony, *First Movement, 18*
   Stravinsky: The Rite of Spring, *Opening Sections, 19*

3   Getting Started: Research   21
Choosing a Topic, 21
Kinds of Topics, 23
What Research Means, 24
Gathering Materials, 25

Places to Start: Print Resources, 26
  Library Catalogs, 26
  Dictionaries and Encyclopedias, 26
  Histories of Music, 28
  Biographies, 30
  Thematic Catalogs, 30
  Articles, 31
  Dissertations, 31
  Scores and Recordings, 32
Places to Start: Electronic Resources, 33
  On-line Library Catalogs, 33
  Databases on CD-ROM, 34
  The Internet, 35
Evaluating Resources, 37
Foreign-Language Resources, 38
When to Stop: How Much Research Is Enough? 38

4   Writing a Research Paper   40
The Outline, 40
  Topic and Thesis, 40
  Introduction, 41
  Body, 42
  Conclusion, 42
  Revising the Outline, 42
Writing the Draft, 43
  Musical Examples, 44
  Diagrams, Graphics, and Tables, 45
  Footnotes, 46
  Bibliography, 48
Revising and Editing the Draft, 50
  Computers and Editing, 50
  Checking Spelling and Grammar, 51
  The Editing Process, 52
Printing, 54
Proofreading, 54
Keep Your File, 55
Plagiarism, 55
Conclusion, 57

5   Questions of Format   59
Format for College Papers, 59
  Paper, 60
  Page Format, 60

Fonts, 61
Spacing, 61
Justification, 61
Page Numbers, 62
Format for Quotations, 62
Short Quotations, 63
Block Quotations, 63
Ellipsis and Editorial Additions, 64
Bibliography and Footnote Form, 65
Books, 66
Dissertations, 70
Articles in Dictionaries and Encyclopedias, 70
Articles in Periodicals, 72
Articles in Collections of Essays, 73
Scores, 73
Sound Recordings, 74
Citing Interviews, Correspondence, and E-Mail, 75
Citing Electronic Resources, 75
Format Issues Related to Writing about Music, 78
Stylistic Periods, 78
Referring to Musical Works, 78
Naming Notes and Keys, 80
Foreign Terms, 81
Musical Examples, 82
Conclusion, 82

6   Other Kinds of Writing Projects   83
The Seminar Presentation, 83
Research, 84
Organizing the Presentation, 84
Tone and Approach, 88
Concert Reports, 88
Purpose, 89
Research, 89
Writing the Report, 90
Program Notes, 91
Purpose, 91
Who Is the Audience? 91
Research, 92
Working within Limits, 93
Special Problems, 94
Texts and Translations, 96
Conclusion, 97

Essay Examinations, 97
  Purpose, 97
  Preparing for Essay Examinations, 98
  How to Proceed, 98
  Common Errors, 99
Conclusion, 101

7   Writing Style   102

Some Basic Ideas about Writing, 102
Kinds of Prose, 104
Tone, 105
The Stance of the Writer, 106
Referring to Yourself, 107
Writing Effective Sentences, 108
  Word Choice, 108
  Word Combinations, 111
  Sentence Structure, 114
Effective Paragraphs, 118
The Effective Essay, 119
  Introduction, 119
  Transitions, 120
  Conclusion, 120
Summary, 121

8   Common Writing Problems   122

Errors in Basic Grammar and Writing, 122
  Incomplete Sentences, 122
  Run-on Sentences, 123
  Agreement: Subject and Verb, 123
  Agreement: Pronoun and Antecedent, 124
  Proper Cases of Pronouns, 126
  Relative Pronouns, 126
  Misplaced Modifiers, 128
  The Split Infinitive, 131
  Mixed Metaphors, 131
Spelling Issues, 132
  Using a Dictionary, 132
  Forming Possessives, 133
  Plurals of Borrowed Latin and Greek Words, 134
  Foreign Words, 134
  Medieval and Renaissance Names, 135

Some Troublesome Word Pairs, 136
    Its and It's, 136
    Your and You're, 136
    Whose and Who's, 137
    Affect and Effect, 137
    Due to and Because of, 137
    Discreet and Discrete, 137
    Fewer and Less, 138
    Principal and Principle, 138
Punctuation, 138
    The Period, 139
    The Comma, 139
    The Semicolon, 141
    The Colon, 142
    Quotation Marks, 142
    The Hyphen, 143
    The Dash, 143
    Parentheses, 144
Special Problems Involved in Writing about Music, 144
    Technical Terms, 144
    Describing Musical Events, 147
Summary, 149

Conclusion 150

Appendix: Sample Paper 152

Index 167

Preface

Since its publication in 1990, this writing guide for undergraduate music majors has proved useful in music departments and schools of music in the United States and Canada. It has been used in academic courses by both music majors and nonmajors. A second edition in 1997 attempted to improve on both the content and the tone of the first edition, and updated the listings of resources useful for research and writing.

PURPOSE OF THE THIRD EDITION

It is now time to publish a third edition of this guide. The information about resources in the second edition is out of date, particularly in view of the appearance of important new print resources, especially the second edition of *The New Grove Dictionary of Music and Musicians,* and the proliferation of Web sites useful for research. In recent years, musicological research has continued to flourish in such areas as cultural and gender studies, areas I deal with more thoroughly in the new section about research. In addition, I am a co-author, with Silvia Herzog, of a new text for beginning graduate students in music, *Introduction to Research in Music,* published by Prentice Hall in 2001. There is, of course, a certain amount of overlap in content between the two books, but also, working on the graduate-level text clarified my thinking on several issues connected with research and writing and led to clearer ways of presenting certain material. Once the necessary changes were made, these new ideas proved useful in this undergraduate guide as well.

There is clearly a greater need than ever for a manual like this. Even though all students now use either their own computers or the sophisticated equipment colleges and universities provide for their use, many students still hand in papers that are actually preliminary drafts in desperate need of revision and proofreading. The irony is that today's word-processing equipment makes revising and editing so much easier than it was in the old days when we used typewriters. I have noticed another strange phenomenon since the advent of personal computers. In all my undergraduate classes in recent years, there have been one or two students with a flair for graphics who hand in papers with marvelous illustrations on the title page; unfortunately, that creativity and skill does not always extend to the papers inside. In fairness, I must point out that in every class there are also some students who have finely honed writing skills, who can argue complex ideas clearly and skillfully, and who produce prose that is a pleasure to read. The expansion in today's college population widens tremendously the gap between the best and the worst students in skills such as critical thinking and persuasive writing. Instructors constantly worry about the difficulty of organizing their courses so that they continue to challenge the best students while still making it possible for less-gifted students to succeed. My hope is that this manual will be of use to all undergraduate students. Students who are already skillful writers can use it as a review, and students who somehow entered college without basic writing skills can also learn some useful things from it. In addition, this guide may continue to be useful for new graduate students who have not had a decent writing course in their undergraduate years or for whom English is a second language.

Another reason for producing a third edition is that the language is still under assault all around us. We are bombarded daily by imprecise and careless language. On television broadcasts of football games, coaches babble at half time about their hopes for a better second half—"We made too many mental errors in the first half. We're gonna have to suck it up, find some people who can step up and go out there and make something happen!" The words sound resolute, but what exactly do they mean? Newscasters talk about neighborhoods "decimated" by floods or fires, and observe, "Hopefully, the rain will end by the weekend." Even leading newspapers, probably relying too heavily on their computers' spell-checking programs, regularly print such gaffes as "waiting with baited breath," "pouring over the records," and "tow the line." By the way, if you don't see any problem with those examples, this guide may be very useful for you—or you might want to check your dictionary. Since the last edition of this book, new clichés have sprouted up, taking over the language like crabgrass. Everywhere English is spoken, "at the end of the day" is used in the sense of "when the dust settles" or "when all is said and done." That last expression, come to think of it, never made much sense either. Some people can't speak two sentences without inserting the ubiquitous "bottom line," "raising the bar," "been there, done that," or the strange-sounding "24/7" meaning "all the time," as in "That guy must practice 24/7!" Others cannot put a sentence together without including one or more of the all-purpose meaningless fillers popular with some groups—"like," "totally," and "y'know."

The point of complaining about the way English is abused all around us is not that we should try to hold back the tide, so to speak, or freeze English into an unchanging, unspoken language like Latin. English has thrived on constant change in its long and tangled history and has absorbed new words from every language around it; it also has a long history of wildly colorful slang. But when you write an academic paper, you are expected to have control over the language and the skill to choose appropriate words and expressions with clarity and precision so that you can communicate your ideas effectively to an academic audience. Good writing has grace and rhythm, and it is a satisfying experience to rebuild and reshape a tangled snarl of awkward expressions until the words flow gracefully and convey exactly what you want to say, with power and persuasion. My fondest hope is that this book will help students to write clear, convincing, persuasive prose on musical topics.

CHANGES IN THE THIRD EDITION

I already mentioned the necessity to update several sections, such as the discussion of new areas of musicological research and new resources for research, both print and electronic. Readers familiar with previous editions will also notice a major reorganization of the material, particularly in two sections. First, it seemed dated to have one chapter on the process of writing a research paper and a separate chapter on using word-processing equipment to produce a paper. For years now, no papers have been produced any other way; for that reason, those two chapters have been combined into one. In the section on writing, it seemed to make better sense to combine several short chapters on style into one longer chapter. The result is that the number of chapters is smaller, although the manual is actually longer, and I hope more useful. Finally, every sentence has been revised and rewritten; I hope that an already useful book has been vastly improved.

OTHER RESOURCES

As I have mentioned already, this manual is directed primarily to undergraduate students. There are several published guides to research and writing designed for graduate music students that deserve mention here, since they may be helpful to undergraduate students as well. Some of these guides deal with issues that are not immediately relevant to undergraduate students, such as special formats for theses and dissertations, but many of the questions they discuss are helpful to students at any level. Among the resources designed for students at the graduate level are the following texts:

Duckles, Vincent H., and Ida Reed. *Music Reference and Research Materials: An Annotated Bibliography,* 5th ed. New York: Schirmer Books, 1997.
Radice, Mark A. *Irvine's Writing about Music,* 3rd ed., revised and enlarged. Portland, OR: Amadeus Press, 1999.

Wingell, Richard, and Silvia Herzog. *Introduction to Research in Music.* Upper Saddle
River, NJ: Prentice Hall, 2001.

A word about these resources is in order. The Duckles and Reed book,
as the title indicates, is an annotated bibliography—a vast list of bibliographical and other resources for research into musical topics. Your music library undoubtedly has a copy in the reference section; browse through it to
get an idea of the astounding variety of musical topics and resources for research into them. Mark Radice's book is a sweeping revision of a classic text
on writing, Demar Irvine's *Writing about Music;* it is designed not only for
students but also for anyone writing about music for publication. Finally,
the Wingell and Herzog book is a newly published textbook for the courses
on research required of new graduate students in music. It includes both a
lengthy discussion of resources for research and a detailed guide to designing and writing a research paper at the graduate level.

There are also several standard guides to writing style. Although these
works do not always discuss the special problems involved in writing about
music at the level of detail we would like, they provide useful information
in matters of appropriate style and format for college papers, as well as for
general publishing. Among the best-known guides are the following:

The Chicago Manual of Style, 14th ed. Chicago and London: University of Chicago
Press, 1993.
Strunk, William, and E. B. White. *The Elements of Style.* New York: Macmillan, 1959.
2nd ed., 1972.
Troyka, Lynn Quitman. *Simon & Schuster Handbook for Writers,* 5th ed. Upper Saddle
River, NJ: Prentice Hall, 1999.
Turabian, Kate L. *A Manual for Writers of Term Papers, Theses, and Dissertations,* 5th
ed., revised and expanded by Bonnie Birtwhistle Honigsblum. Chicago and
London: University of Chicago Press, 1987.

The Turabian manual is a standard reference work, recommended in
many college and university courses. Although Turabian includes a few brief
sections on the special problems of writing about music, it is most useful as
a general guide to writing graduate research papers. Turabian follows closely
The Chicago Manual of Style, a large, very detailed guide, and a standard reference work for writers, editors, proofreaders, and publishers. Both Turabian
and the *Chicago Manual* include detailed guides to the style of citation used
in humanities papers as well as the author-date citation style used in the natural and social sciences. The *Chicago Manual* is the bible of the publishing
world; the size of the book and the number of editions testify to its importance. On issues of style in this guide, I have generally used the *Chicago Manual* as the final word; in those cases where I disagree with its recommendations, I have made a note to that effect. *The Chicago Manual of Style* publishes

a new edition roughly every ten years; the fifteenth edition is expected in 2003. The publishers also manage a Web site that deals with questions not covered in the latest printed edition; the Web site is particularly helpful in the somewhat confusing new area of citing electronic resources. The book by Strunk and White is an inexpensive paperback that discusses a few selected questions of writing style; it belongs in the personal library of anyone who cares about writing precise and careful English. The *Simon & Schuster Handbook* is a useful compendium of the details of correct grammar and writing style, reviewing everything that would be covered in a good college course on writing. Finally, students should be aware that their instructors or institutions may have chosen Turabian or another guide as their official style guide; thus, the detailed recommendations contained in this handbook may not be appropriate for all classes.

HOW TO USE THIS BOOK

This guide is not intended to be read cover to cover. It offers practical advice in several areas, including writing a research paper, writing style, general writing problems, and the special challenges of writing about music. Although it is aimed primarily at the undergraduate music major, some graduate students may profit from a review of the process of writing a paper or from the chapters on effective writing. Although some students may find some of the comments and suggestions too elementary, all the questions discussed—even the most basic ones—are included because they still cause problems for many students. Familiarize yourself with the book's organization, study the table of contents, and skim through the whole book so that you are aware of the areas it covers. In the future, when you are involved in a writing project, you will then be able to locate the material that may be of practical use to you.

The book is divided into four large sections. Chapters 1 and 2 discuss the issue of writing about music. Chapters 3, 4, and 5 cover every stage of the research paper process, from choosing a topic through doing research, outlining, writing the draft, and editing and revising, as well as questions of format. Chapter 6 discusses other kinds of writing about music that you may be involved in—seminar presentations, concert reports, program notes, and essay examinations. Chapters 7 and 8 treat writing in general—principles of style, effective writing, and common problems. The concluding section offers some last words of advice. In the Appendix is a sample paper, newly chosen for this third edition, which you can use as a model, and some questions to aid you in your analysis of the paper. Skip around the book and use what you need. My hope is that all students will find helpful information somewhere in this book. At the least, the book should direct them to other resources where they can find the help they seek.

CONCLUSION

This book is intended to serve as a practical introductory guide. It does not pretend to present the last word on all issues involved in writing about music. Rather, it is intended to be helpful in a few important areas, especially to the student facing the task of writing a paper on a musical topic. If the book helps students to produce papers that are stronger, clearer, and more convincing, it will have justified its existence.

Finally, I should again thank some people who supplied ideas and material for this book. First, I am indebted to Norwell F. Therien, Jr., former Acquisitions Editor in Humanities at Prentice Hall, who conceived the idea for this book and supervised the production of the first edition, and his successor Christopher Johnson, who fulfilled the same functions for the second and third editions. I am also indebted to several reviewers who offered thoughtful criticism of the second edition and suggestions for revisions: Dr. Katherine Powers, California State University–Fullerton; Dr. Jeanne Belfy, Boise State University; Dr. Eldonna L. May, University of Michigan–Dearborn; and Dr. Mary Wischusen, Wayne State University. Next, I thank my colleagues in Music History at the University of Southern California; over the years, we have continually discussed student papers, writing problems, and ways to help students write better. Finally, I must thank the hundreds of students whose papers I have read and criticized and who have contributed to this book, directly and indirectly. I hope it will prove useful to them and to their present and future colleagues.

Richard J. Wingell

Writing about Music

Writing about Music

WHY WE WRITE ABOUT MUSIC

As a student of music, you will certainly face the challenging task of writing about music during the course of your academic career. You will be expected to write projects of various sorts, research papers, program notes for your recitals, essay questions in music history examinations, and perhaps a presentation in a seminar or even a senior thesis. If you choose to go on to graduate work in music, the writing demands will increase exponentially, including many more research papers, probably a lecture-recital, and perhaps a thesis or culminating project of some kind. It is impossible to predict the various kinds of writing you might find yourself doing in your professional life: program notes for concerts and recordings, articles in periodicals, reviews of concerts or recordings, and work connected with various sorts of Web sites, to name just a few. Writing about music is not something you can choose to do or not to do; you will spend considerable time both now and later working at this complex task. It therefore behooves us to begin this guide with some thoughts on the special challenges of writing about music.

Throughout the history of music, there have been vocal opponents of the whole idea of writing about music. These people feel that music speaks for itself and that words are inadequate to describe musical events. Even in the nineteenth century, with all its artistic manifestos, arguments about the directions music should take, and endless discussions of music's capacity to tell stories, stir feelings, or express philosophical ideas, there were still those who insisted that music must speak for itself and that writing about it is pointless. In our own day, many composers resist the attempts of commentators to explain their music, preferring to let the music speak for them. Why would someone go to the effort of writing about this complex and difficult art? What purpose is served by crafting clear prose about music?

Sometimes the purpose of writing about music is clear and straightforward. The goal in writing program notes, for example, is to help the members of the audience understand the music better and thus increase their enjoyment of the concert. Sometimes one writes about music to establish one's credentials as a knowledgeable musician. It seems obvious that a performer who can speak intelligently of the historical background and style of a piece of music is a more competent musician than a performer who may be able to play the notes but cannot say anything intelligent about the music beyond "I like it," "I don't like it," or "It's hard." Further, one might write about a piece of music to explain one's analytic understanding of how the work is put together and what gives it coherence, logic, and syntax. One may write to show how a musical work is connected to a particular culture and its concerns, or to further the aims of some powerful group. One may also want to show the connection between a musical work and the art and literature that flourished in the culture at the same time. Professors sometimes assign writing projects to encourage students to apply the ideas discussed in class to various musical works, a more thoughtful and demanding task than simply absorbing what the professor says and repeating it back in an examination. Such papers are exercises in what psychologists call second-order learning—that is, the ability to apply newly acquired insight and skills to new experiences. One might also write to convey the results of one's historical, biographical, or cultural research on a musical topic. Musicological research, as we shall see, is concerned with areas other than analysis. It also includes studies in biography, cultural background, connections with the other arts, performance practice issues, the way different cultures and different eras deal with music from the past (what the Germans call *Rezeptionsgeschichte*, or "reception history"), and critical approaches borrowed from literary theory. Writing is the only way we can communicate the results of our research.

THE SPECIAL CHALLENGES OF WRITING ABOUT MUSIC

It is not easy to write convincingly about music. Music is a nonverbal art; it often seems to speak directly to feelings deep within us that are difficult to put into words. For that reason, music has always been a crucial part of religious rituals, patriotic ceremonies, and solemn occasions of all sorts, civic or private. Even when music accompanies a text, as in art song or opera, we find it difficult to express exactly what the music "says" beyond what the text says, or what the music adds to the words. We assume that music adds something to a text, because, unless the composer has something to say beyond what the poet has said in the text, there is little point in setting a text in the first place. Often we feel that a musical setting captures the feeling of a text with remarkable exactness, that in some way it is exactly right for that text, but it is difficult to explain that conviction in prose. The very nature of music resists attempts to verbalize about it. On the other hand, when we finally arrive at a clear vision of a work, or when we have strong ideas about a work's uniqueness or historical importance, or its power as a cultural statement, we want to communicate our ideas, insights, and opinions. Words are the only means we have to communicate what we want to say about the music we love.

Besides the inherent difficulty of writing about music, there are extrinsic factors that make it more difficult. Some performers seem to approach all music simply as a challenge to their technique, as if the only significant music consisted of solos for their particular instrument. Their attitude seems to be, "Spare me the lectures—just give me the score and I'll take it home and learn it." Perhaps they learned that attitude from their studio teachers; unfortunately, some teachers concentrate almost entirely on technical issues and give little attention to analytic or stylistic understanding.

Outside the specialized world of musicians, society's attitudes toward music also affect us. Our culture thinks of music as comforting background noise, an atmosphere one creates for oneself, a sort of sonic wallpaper. According to this view, no one has any right to question anyone else's musical taste; like religious or political convictions, musical taste is regarded as a personal matter and a dangerous topic for discussion. Qualitative judgments are not welcome in this atmosphere. The fan of heavy metal, country music, alternative rock, or rap, for example, will not tolerate opinions that one sort of music is "better" or "more worthwhile" than any other; questions of quality are regarded as pedantic, oppressive, and offensive. Many people cannot imagine that there can be any thoughtful discussion of a musical experience beyond rudimentary approval or disapproval. In this atmosphere, it is difficult to argue logically and convincingly about issues of musical style or quality.

INAPPROPRIATE WAYS TO WRITE ABOUT MUSIC

Because it is difficult to write about music, some writers fill their pages with irrelevant discussions, perhaps resorting to diversionary tactics to avoid the challenge of actually discussing the music. We have all read examples of these approaches to writing about music. Please note that the following examples of bad writing are not direct quotations but my own paraphrases of prose I have read.

Sometimes, especially in program notes and CD booklets, one finds overly precious descriptions of musical events, sentences like the following.

> The violas insist on interrupting with their own little theme, but the woodwinds are not impressed and continue chattering among themselves. Finally, the brasses put a stop to the argument by drowning out everyone else and restoring order.
>
> The introduction has no thematic connection to the movement proper, but provides a delightful aperitif to what follows.

These fanciful metaphors tell us little about the music.

Sometimes, sentimental or overly picturesque descriptions take the place of serious discussion. Returning themes "dispel the gloom and chaos of the preceding section," or "The light of hope finally dawns as we approach the triumphant final section." Themes "babble," "chatter," "argue," "soar," or "shout." This picturesque language provides little of substance to the reader who wants to understand the music better.

Another tendency is to treat all music as programmatic, regardless of the style in question or the composer's intent. It is perfectly all right to let one's imagination wander and conjure up colorful pictures or scenes as one listens to music, even absolute or abstract music. In fact, it would be fascinating if we could magically project on a screen the images that pass through the minds of a concert audience during a performance. Sharing one's fantasies, however, hardly fulfills the writer's responsibility to discuss musical matters in a serious paper. One student, in a paper analyzing a concerto grosso, included the information that Baroque music always conjures up images of royal processions in her mind. That bit of shared information is irrelevant to a discussion of the music.

There is a nineteenth-century description of the opening of Brahms's First Symphony that goes on at some length about "the cosmic questions posed by the philosophic C." The opening of that symphony is certainly one of the most dramatic opening gestures in the symphonic literature, but "cosmic questions"? If you want to convey the power of that opening, you have to say something about what actually happens in the music. Whatever words you might choose, the important elements to discuss include the relentless pounding of the pedal C and the contrary motion between the upper instruments as they move away in chromatic steps from their initial unison C. Take a moment and try to describe that opening in your own words; you will find that mention of the crucial musical events is the only way to keep the statement from lapsing into Romantic dreaming or programmatic nonsense.

A related approach tries to explain all music through events in the composer's life. Beethoven's deafness, for example, occupies altogether too much space in discussions of his later music; it is easier to write about his affliction than to discuss the puzzling, fragmented style of his late works. There is a published discussion of Mozart's Piano Concerto in B-flat, K. 595, that relates this final concerto to Mozart's supposed feelings as he neared the end of his short life. The writer describes the serene slow movement as "suffused with the soft glow of evening," or words to that effect, and hears resignation and a longing for death in every note. The connection with Mozart's feelings in his last days is hard to justify, since many of his earlier slow movements are equally serene. Besides, Mozart hardly seems the sort of person who would approach his untimely death with an "evening glow" of resignation. Nineteenth-century writers loved to treat Mozart as a tragic Romantic hero, but the emphasis on the tragic side of his life tells us little about Mozart's real genius or about his music. Sometimes details of a composer's life, such as an important friendship, a new position, or connections with artists or writers can shed helpful light on his or her evolving musical style. One must always bear in mind, however, that unhappy composers can write happy music, and composers whose lives are dull can write turbulent, passionate music. Examples come readily to mind. Bartók's *Concerto for Orchestra,* for example, is an exuberant, exciting work; it hardly sounds like the work of a composer who at that time was dying of leukemia in an American hospital, exiled from war-torn Europe, impoverished, depressed, and discouraged. Richard Strauss in his private life was, we are told, a henpecked, middle-class German, but his tone poems embody all the sweep, grandeur, and ardent heroism of late Romanticism.

The lives of composers and their interaction with the culture around them are, of course, endlessly fascinating to us and worthy material for research and writing. Biographical studies are one of the traditional areas of musicological research, and there is great interest at present in studying the relationship between societies such as Nazi Germany and the Soviet Union and the composers who lived, willingly or unwillingly, under those repressive regimes. What I am saying, however, is that composers' lives, or particular events in them, do not necessarily tell us all we want to know about their music.

There are other tempting but inappropriate approaches to writing about music. Some students think they have said all there is to say about a piece of music when they have reported the musical events in the order in which they occur. You surely have read—or perhaps written—prose like the following.

> The first sixteen measures of the development section are based on the first theme, and gradually reduce the musical idea to the first phrase, and finally to just the opening flourish, which moves through several key areas. The next thirty-two measures continue the modulatory process, after which a dominant pedal prepares for the recapitulation.

Although this "one-thing-after-another" approach appears to be neutral, objective, and scientific, it is not real analysis, as we shall see in Chapter 2. Unless the music happens to be organized as a series of unrelated events, as in some twentieth-century styles, merely compiling a list of events avoids taking a position on what is important in the music, what unifies the work and gives it coherence, and what makes it different from other works in the same style or genre. The listing of musical events is certainly a vast improvement over gushing prose about babbling brooks, chattering woodwinds, the imagined feelings of the composer at the time, or the fevered dreams of the listener's imagination. It is only a beginning, however, and does not complete the task of describing the music. Some great music is the result of enormously complicated compositional processes. The first step in understanding complex genres such as isorhythmic motets, eighteenth-century fugues, or serial and pan-serial compositions is the sometimes arduous task of observing and listing all the elements of the compositional process—permutations of the *talea* and *color,* appearances of the fugue subject in all its different versions, or occurrences of the row in all its permutations. Taking the composition apart in this way is often a daunting and fascinating process, and it may very well be a necessary first step, but explaining the compositional process of a piece of music is not the same as making a statement about its style. The complex web of events and design elements is important but does not really explain the style of the work, as a few examples will illustrate. Schoenberg's serial works are quite different from Webern's; if you listen carefully, you can hear that many serial works by Schoenberg are actually organized in nontonal versions of standard classical forms. In the same way, a trained ear can distinguish between a *cantus firmus* Mass by Dufay and one by Josquin des Prez, or between a sonata-allegro movement by Haydn and one by Mozart. Zeroing in on the unique qualities or the individual essence of a great musical work and then clearly expressing that insight is perhaps the most difficult part of writing about music.

Another error is anachronistic analysis—trying to understand or describe music of one era by using the analytic tools and categories appropriate to music from a different era altogether, or forcing a piece of music into the wrong stylistic mold. The concepts of structure and key areas that work perfectly well for analyzing Haydn symphonies will not be of much use in analyzing a motet by Guillaume de Machaut, a song by Charles Ives, or aleatoric music by John Cage. Students often try to analyze early music by using their recently acquired vocabulary of analytic terms appropriate for tonal music from the eighteenth and nineteenth centuries. When grappling with music that does not have antecedent and consequent phrases, clear key areas, obvious dominant–tonic cadences, or familiar classical forms, they sometimes try to force the music to fit the wrong style. Clearly, each musical work has to be judged on its own terms, against the background of the cultural and stylistic norms of its own day.

It is important to realize that stylistic analysis is not an exact science, with quantifiable issues and definite answers. Nor is it a permanently fixed, unchanging methodology; several new approaches to analysis have emerged in this century, each with its own contribution to the understanding of music, its organization, and its meaning. On the one hand are the analytic systems of Heinrich Schenker, Paul Hindemith, and Allen Forte; these methods of analysis emphasize the structure of a work or its materials and methods and seek to establish a single system that will work for all styles of music. Musicologists, on the other hand, generally approach music from a wider perspective.

MUSICOLOGICAL RESEARCH AND WRITING

Some musicologists continue to work in the traditional kinds of research. Analytical research focuses on the music itself and discusses issues of evolving genres and styles. Archival research searches for information on the musical life of a particular place and time, the venues in which music was performed, and the forces that were available to perform the music. Biographical research uncovers information on the lives of composers and performers, shedding light on why and how they produced their music. Cultural research connects music with the historical and artistic trends at work in the surrounding culture.

In recent decades, musicological research has greatly widened its sphere of activity. Cultural studies have expanded to include areas such as reception history, which studies the ways in which various cultures have understood and responded to particular works, either works from the past or contemporary works, or how societies have used works from the past to support their own aims. In addition, musicology has borrowed the concept of "deconstruction" from literary theory and begun pursuing the concept that any work of art, programmatic or absolute, makes a statement about the power structure or culture from which it comes. Armed with new methodologies, we can learn to "read" those statements. This concept has also led to such specialized types of research as feminist criticism and gay studies. The modernist/postmodernist debate goes on in music as well as in the other arts, and at times the arguments have turned into ringing manifestos and heated debates. Still, all these new approaches have produced thoughtful and provocative studies that broaden, rather than replace, traditional methods of musical analysis and research.

Some undergraduate students may be asked to do these new kinds of research in their classes; the option of choosing one of these new approaches for a research project will certainly be part of graduate work for those who choose to go on to that level. The next chapter will illustrate different kinds of research as they might be applied to selected musical works—stylistic analysis first, since that is presumably the main sort of research undergraduates will be asked to do, and then suggestions about other directions one might pursue, taking those works as a starting point. The important thing to realize at this point is that, whatever focus one chooses, any sound research on a musical topic must always start from an understanding of the music itself. Stylistic analysis and an understanding of changing musical styles form the essential starting point for any serious research. Otherwise, we are back in the world of fanciful imagination or personal reaction, not something one can argue logically or intellectually.

We move on, then, to a consideration of some striking musical works from different eras and discussion of ways in which these individual works can suggest possible avenues for research and topics for papers.

CHAPTER 2

Analysis and Research

This chapter continues our discussion of stylistic analysis of music, as musicologists use the term, and attempts to illustrate the concept through brief discussion of some particularly interesting musical works. In addition, for each of these works, I will try to show how the researcher might develop other directions and topics for research, moving outward in concentric circles from a single piece of music. We begin with a discussion of stylistic analysis.

ANALYSIS

In theory courses, the term *analysis* usually refers either to harmonic and structural analysis of pieces from the so-called standard-practice period (1750–1900) or to new systems of analysis developed in the twentieth century. Music historians, on the other hand, generally use the term to mean stylistic analysis, and they study musical works in the broader context of changing historical styles. All composers work within a stylistic context; they either accept the stylistic assumptions and conventions of their time or consciously depart from those conventions, creating new musical styles. Therefore, meaningful analysis ought to be based on a clear understanding of the stylistic developments that form the context in which a particular work appeared. We cannot appreciate the unique aspects of a particular work until we understand the principles that guide the music of the period. Therefore, musicology often concentrates its effort on defining the principles of a particular style.

No matter how one defines analysis, it certainly involves more than mere description, chord counting, or listing of events. True analysis implies insight into how the music is conceived and organized. To gain that insight, one may have to start with list-making activities as described in the last chapter, but those activities are only the preliminaries to analysis; after events are identified and sorted out, the real work of analysis begins. One must decide which events are significant, which are not, and how the work relates to a more general historical style; only then can one decide which elements of the work are standard practice for the time and which are innovative. In other words, analysis is not really an objective, scientific activity; it involves a creative mind and artistic judgment, as well as the ability to create an analytic hypothesis and the appropriate means to test that hypothesis. I should also point out that analysis should include among its tools the ear as well as the eye; if analysis is to arrive at the basic elements that hold a work together and give it unity, our final view of the work ought to be audible. Music is, after all, a sonic art, not a visual one, and the marks on a page of score are only representations of the sounds the composer chose and the way they are organized.

In a similar vein, analysis of a musical work, as we saw in the last chapter, is different from understanding the compositional process involved. Discovering all the permutations of a fugue subject or deciphering every chord in a highly chromatic tone poem is not the same as understanding the style of the work. Even the laborious task of locating all the permutations of the row in a twelve-tone work is different from stylistic analysis. Schoenberg's serial works are stylistically quite distinct from those of Berg, Webern, or Boulez. The issue of compositional process may even be peripheral to the question of style, since the structure and coherence of a work often result from entirely different considerations. Many of Schoenberg's twelve-tone works, for example, are organized in recognizable versions of classical structures, such as sonata-allegro or rondo. Even the seams between sections are often articulated through familiar classical means, such as melodic and rhythmic cadence, change of texture, or change of instrumentation, which have little to do with row permutations. Knowledge of the compositional process can certainly shed light on the organization of a work; Schoenberg viewed the serial process as the fundamental source of the work's unity and coherence, since the common material is the basis of the extended work. Still, the task of analysis involves more than awareness of compositional process.

Analysis, then, is something other than harmonic and structural analysis of works from the standard-practice period, making lists, or understanding the compositional process. Most historians define analysis as insight into how a work is organized, what gives it logic and coherence, and how it relates to the important stylistic developments of its time.

QUESTIONS TO CONSIDER

To begin the process of musical analysis, one should consider several basic questions. Is this particular work organized as a coherent unit? If so, what is the basis of its coherence? What makes this work a unified whole? Is it based on one of the traditional structural patterns, such as sonata-allegro, minuet and trio, or theme and variations, or does it have some other form? We can always assume that musical works are based on some principle of organization; unless at some level we sense some logic and coherence in a work, we dismiss it as random, inartistic, and a waste of our time and attention. Identifying the musical means by which the composer has built in unity and coherence is the most important step in analysis.

Another basic question in stylistic analysis is how a particular work relates to the stylistic developments of its time. Is it a venture into completely new territory, or does it build on established styles? Is it a further refinement of a style in which the composer has worked previously, or is the composer experimenting with new stylistic ideas? In what way has the composer worked out his or her own individual version of an established style? Further, is there evidence that the composer was influenced by another composer? Claims of another composer's influence are difficult to support; similarity of style is not enough in itself to justify such a claim, since there are several other possible explanations for such similarity. The line of influence may run in the opposite direction, or both may have been influenced by a third composer or a pervasive style of the period. It is difficult to prove influence from the music alone, unless we have the composer's own words or some other historical evidence that establishes a connection. Within these limits, however, the question of influence and the other general questions listed earlier are ways to approach the crucial issue of where a work fits in the overall history of a style.

Another possible direction to pursue when beginning an analysis project is relating a particular work to the surrounding culture and contemporary developments in the other arts. At some times in history, the connections between music and the other arts are particularly obvious. French art songs of the early twentieth century, for example, cannot be understood without reference to the symbolist literary movement that produced the evocative texts that determined the composers' musical choices and led them to create a new musical style. Likewise, the songs of Schoenberg and Berg cannot be understood without some understanding of the expressionist movement in German art and literature. In fact, we often use terms borrowed from the world of the visual arts, such as impressionism and expressionism, to describe musical styles, and we cannot discuss expressionism in music without first understanding what the term means in its original context. Programmatic music clearly cannot be analyzed without some reference to the story or picture the music is trying to depict.

The question of cultural context affects all music, not just those musical styles obviously influenced by the visual or literary arts. The physical setting in which music was performed, the audience for whom it was intended, the context that called for a performance, and the way a particular society viewed the role of composer or performer all affect questions of stylistic development. Understanding a musical work may involve research into these sociological questions. We need to be aware of concert life in earlier ages, the performing forces composers had at their disposal, and the context in which music was performed. To understand the cantatas of Bach, for example, we must first understand that they were designed to be performed in a small space as part of a four-hour Sunday service, and we cannot understand the music without some sense of the religious movement known as Pietism and the effect it had on religious ideas and attitudes in Bach's church. The better we understand the original purpose of a musical work, the audience for whom it was intended, and the circumstances of its first performance, the better prepared we are to make sense of the music.

Another fundamental question to raise in the early stages of an analysis project is the composer's intent. Since composers write their music for many different reasons, understanding their motivation may very well be the key to understanding the music they produce.

Sometimes a composer writes music for a particular occasion, and that special purpose affects the style of the music he writes. A famous example of music for a special occasion is *Nuper rosarum flores,* a motet by Guillaume Dufay and one of the masterpieces of the early Renaissance. The piece is remarkably complex. Not only does it utilize an archaic compositional process that goes back to Machaut and the fourteenth century; it goes beyond Machaut by utilizing two isorhythmic tenors that move in canon at the fifth. Of course, one could analyze the motet by working from the score alone, but it makes more sense to see the work in its historical context. The motet was commissioned in 1436 for the dedication of Brunelleschi's new dome for the cathedral in Florence. This ceremony was a major event in Renaissance Italy; the Pope was in attendance, and the fact that Dufay was selected to compose the music for this occasion is a sign of the high regard in which he was held. Recent scholarship has put forth the theory that the double-tenor structure of Dufay's piece was intended to mirror in music the mathematical elements of Brunelleschi's bold design for the large unsupported dome. The motet may also have been intended to reflect the proportions of Solomon's Temple as described in the Bible; the two tenors are arranged in a mathematical proportion that duplicates the proportions of Solomon's Temple. In other words, the circumstances explain the structure of the music, and it would be a mistake to treat this piece as if it were an ordinary motet.

Composers have often written music for a particular performer, and that circumstance should help us understand those works. Compositional choices may be based on the particular talents of the performers for whom the works are intended, and the question of instrumental idiom may be a central question to raise in the analytical process.

Sometimes the composer's main purpose is to experiment with new materials or structures. Much of the music composed since 1945 should be approached with a clear awareness of the composer's purpose. George Crumb, for example, often combines in his music ideas borrowed from Oriental music, ritual, astronomy, and drama. Works of this period, in which the composer sometimes creates a new style or structure for a single work, must be analyzed in terms of what the composer intended to accomplish. If a composer has organized a particular work around mathematical structures, has ordered all the elements serially, or has integrated musical ideas from other cultures into Western structures, we cannot analyze or appreciate the work except in those terms.

Sometimes, on the other hand, a composer may be refining an established style, and the key to analyzing his work is to view it against the background of that established style. That is the case with much of the music from the standard-practice period. When we approach a Mozart symphony, we know how to proceed, because we have some understanding of the principles of classical structure. When a composer moves from one style to another, as Stravinsky did in his later years, we obviously have to be aware of that change and must not try to analyze his serial works using the same criteria we would use to analyze his neoclassical works.

Finally, if a composer has written a programmatic work, we cannot adequately appreciate the music without some understanding of the program. The same holds true for text setting in song and opera; the complex relationship between text and music is one of the major questions to consider in the process of analysis.

In short, we should judge musical works against the background of what the composer was trying to do. To ignore available information about the composer's intent is to deprive ourselves of a useful guide to the directions the analysis should take. Sometimes we are already armed with an understanding of the composer's intent, as in the case of Mozart or Beethoven. In other cases, we may have to begin our analysis by study of the composer's ideas and aims so that we can approach the music as he or she approached it and avoid using inappropriate criteria in our study of the work.

We will now look at some specific works and the analytical approaches that would be appropriate for studying them, as well as other directions for research that these works suggest.

EXAMPLES OF WORKS AND RESEARCH DIRECTIONS

The following works are readily available in standard anthologies of music and can be found in any music library. It would be helpful to have the scores at hand as you read this section so that you can follow the discussion and decide for yourself which approaches seem most fruitful.

Gesualdo: "Moro, lasso"

This famous madrigal is an example of Gesualdo's idiosyncratic style. As you first glance at the score, several aspects of the musical style strike you immediately. The first is the strange chromaticism in the setting of certain phrases—"Moro, lasso," "ahi, che m'ancide," "O dolorosa sorte," and "ahi, mi da morte." We know that in the sixteenth century, madrigal composers were concerned with musical rhetoric—that is, finding appropriate musical ways to depict the striking words and ideas of the text. Clearly, the way to approach this piece is from the point of view of text setting, starting with the Italian text and considering each example of word painting. The words "Moro, lasso," for example, are set to a chromatically descending phrase in the low range; the music seems particularly apt for the words "I die, I languish." There are several chordal, chromatic sections that resemble the opening phrase; the texts in those sections focus on pain and death. Alternating with them are polyphonic sections in diatonic style, which set the more hopeful lines such as "e chi me può dar vita" ("she who could give me life").

You might also focus on the details of the chromatic passages—for example, the composer's pattern of combining parallel chromatic descent with what later theory would call root movement by thirds. You might discuss the chromatic passages in light of the modal theory of the time. You might also focus on overall structure. Note that the structure of the piece is formed by the alternation of the two different styles and the repetition of contrasting passages. Because of the composer's tendency to alternate sections in wildly contrasting styles, you might argue that the style lacks overall unity and coherence. Whatever direction you take, text setting and "madrigalisms" would certainly be among the first questions to pursue.

It is easy to use this piece as a starting point for research topics that are not exclusively analytical. One interesting line of research would be to determine who performed these difficult works. We know from contemporary accounts that they were sung with one voice on each part, and that the soprano parts, and perhaps the alto parts, were sung by women, not by the professional choirboys who sang in the court chapels. Who these women were and how they achieved this virtuoso level of vocal training is an important question. You could also explore Gesualdo's texts. Gesualdo chose not to set the texts by the poets favored by his contemporaries—Petrarch, Guarini, Tasso, and Marino. His madrigals therefore tip the balance in favor of music over text and do not achieve the same delicate equilibrium between text and music that we see in most of the madrigals by Marenzio, Monteverdi, and Giaches de Wert. The contexts for performance of madrigals and the constitution of the audience would be another interesting area to investigate. How audiences reacted to the texts of these pieces and their constant harping on the "sweet pain" of love is another interesting cultural question.

J. S. Bach: Opening Chorus of Cantata No. 80,
Ein' feste Burg ist unser Gott

The obvious first step in an analytical study of this chorus, as is usually the case in the choruses of Bach's chorale cantatas, is to compare the source melody of the traditional chorale with the complex counterpoint that Bach constructed from it. Analysis must begin with the chorale tune with which Bach began; the unadorned tune is found in the soprano line of the final number of the cantata. The key to the structure of this chorus is that Bach uses the chorale tune in two different ways. First, the choral parts constitute a chorale motet—that is, Bach uses each phrase of the chorale tune, modified but still recognizable, as the subject for imitative entries in all the voices. Each phrase in turn is treated this way. This is an old technique, one we associate with the motets and paraphrase Masses of Josquin des Prez. The melody is not quoted literally but is given new rhythmic shape and amplified by added notes, just as Renaissance composers paraphrased chant melodies when they used them as imitative subjects in their motets. At the end of each imitative section, the orchestra presents the same phrase of the chorale in a different way—in literal form, in long notes, called cantus firmus style. In addition, these literal quotations of the chorale phrases in long notes are set canonically between the upper and lower instruments of the orchestra, at a rhythmic distance of one measure. Once one grasps the two ways Bach uses each phrase of the chorale, one understands the whole chorus, since the composer continues this process throughout the chorus. Read through the chorus and see if you can follow the progress of the chorale motet; the orchestra's quotations of the chorale phrases in cantus firmus style clearly mark the end of each imitative section. In addition, the structure of the chorus duplicates the *AAB* structure of the chorale. Other topics one might consider are the relationship of this huge first chorus to the other movements and the overall structure of the cantata. One might also contrast this chorus with an opening chorus organized differently, such as the first chorus of Cantata No. 140, *Wachet auf, ruft uns die Stimme.*

Again it is easy to imagine different kinds of research suggested by this work. One interesting question is an editorial one. The copies and parts that serve as the basis for editions of this work exist in two versions. One uses oboes and the bass strings as the instruments that announce the chorale phrases in cantus firmus style and in canon at the end of each choral section. The other version, introduced after Bach's lifetime, uses trumpets rather than oboes, and adds the kettledrums that regularly accompany trumpets in the Baroque orchestra. In the nineteenth century, when the editors of the *Bach-Gesellschaft-Ausgabe* prepared an edition of this work, they combined these two versions, so that the chorale phrases are played by both oboes and trumpets; the more recent edition in the *Neue-Bach-Ausgabe* includes only the oboes. Tracing the origin of the version for trumpets and drums would be an interesting research project.

Cultural issues surround this work as well. One could study the Pietist movement and its effect on Bach's career as a church musician. It is interesting to note, for instance, that extreme Pietists were opposed to all liturgy and ritual and believed that they did not need pastors to tell them how to interpret the Gospels; under that version of Pietism, Bach's elaborate church music would have no place. On the other hand, had the ideas of Pietism not shaped to some extent the piety of the churches where Bach worked, his deeply personal responses to the Gospel readings of the day, the main reason why we still listen to his church music, would not have been welcome. One could also investigate the work's reception history; this cantata, based on a chorale ascribed to Luther himself and performed on Reformation Sunday, came to be associated with a militant spirit that was not the primary sentiment the composer had in mind when he wrote it. Finally, questions about performance practice, as usual, yield a fruitful area for investigation; some modern scholars are convinced from contemporary evidence that these cantatas—in fact, all of Bach's sacred music—were performed with one voice on each part, a far cry from the giant choral-orchestral performances and recordings we are familiar with.

Mozart: Concerto for Piano and Orchestra in C Minor, K. 491, First Movement

In this work, the researcher is on the familiar ground of standard-practice analysis, dealing with familiar elements such as key areas, thematic repetition, the development process, and classical structures. What this particular movement illustrates is the variety possible within standard classical forms. Structural analysis shows that this movement does not follow the double-exposition version of sonata-allegro structure that some textbooks describe as the model for the first movement of a classical concerto. Many commentators view this movement as an example of ritornello form rather than a sonata-allegro structure. Look through the whole movement. Does the solo piano ever play the first theme? Do the key areas work out as you would expect in a classical sonata-allegro movement in the minor mode? Structural issues would certainly seem to be the main focus for an analysis of this movement. In addition, some commentators view this particular concerto as an example of Mozart's darker, Beethovenian side, in contrast to the sunnier, gentler spirit of some of his other piano concertos. A comparative analysis contrasting this concerto with another one, perhaps the Concerto in A Major, K. 488, would be an interesting project.

Related to structural analysis are two other areas worthy of study—instrumental idiom and orchestration. Mozart used the piano not only as a solo instrument but also as a sort of third choir added to the classical orchestra of strings and winds. Thus, for example, the piano sometimes plays an accompanimental role while solo winds pass around the themes, and over the course of the movement, piano, strings, and winds are deployed in every possible combination. One could also study the pianos Mozart would have played and the effect their particular sound and color would have on the performance. One might also investigate the occasions, venues, and audiences for performances of concertos as opposed to those for performances of symphonic music. Finally, connections and differences between the idea of the concerto in the Classical and Romantic periods would be another fruitful area of study.

Verdi: *Otello*, Act I, Scene 3

The love duet between Otello and Desdemona at the end of Act I of Verdi's *Otello* is both stunning music and effective theater, a moving finale to the first act. The opera opens with a famous storm scene, followed by Otello's triumphant return from a victory over the Turks; a celebration follows, during which Iago sets the plot in motion by getting Cassio drunk and goading him into a fight so that Otello will punish him with imprisonment. Then everyone else leaves the stage, and Desdemona welcomes home her triumphant warrior. The extended love scene that closes the act is one of the high points of the opera and can be studied from several points of view. The musical style is richer and more complex than the style we associate with Verdi's earlier operas. We are immediately struck by the delicately beautiful orchestration, filled with careful and unusual effects. The harmonic idiom, marked by frequent modulations and enharmonic shifts, is also strikingly different from that of Verdi's earlier works. Although some commentators see the structure of a traditional *scena* in this duet, the music seems more continuous and flowing than in Verdi's earlier works. The climax of the scene is the "un bacio" motive, which will return at the tragic close of the opera. Besides analysis of these musical details, one might undertake a comparative analysis. There is a clear shift in style between Verdi's earlier operas and his late works, *Otello* and *Falstaff*. One might try to identify common stylistic traits in these two late works and contrast them with earlier works.

A fascinating nonanalytical topic is the change in the plot and the characters resulting from the cuts Boito made in the process of transforming Shakespeare's play into a libretto. One obvious example is Desdemona. Because Boito cut the entire first act of Shakespeare's play, which establishes Desdemona's strength and independence, the opera portrays her as a typical nineteenth-century heroine, victimized and helpless. The issue of changes in the characters is not just a question of text, because characterization is presented through musical means as well. Iago, for example, is presented differently in his amazing "Credo" number than he is in the play, where his motivation is subtler and more puzzling. When Boito and Verdi adapted the play, which has its own shape and and flow, into another medium, change was inevitable; music has its own rules of structure and flow. One might also compare this adaptation with Verdi's other adaptations of Shakespeare's plays—*Macbeth* and *Falstaff*.

It would also be interesting to study how *Otello* was received. The audience was quite familiar with Verdi's earlier singer-centered style, made up of separate numbers, each with its own climactic high notes and triumphant cadences. I wonder how the first audience reacted to this new and somewhat

Wagnerian style, in which the singers' lines weave through a complex orchestral fabric, and the music is not divided into separate numbers that have clear starting points and obvious cadences with built-in pauses for applause. Finally, the central role of Othello the Moor raises the question of racism and how audiences of various periods and cultures have responded to the tragic hero, who is presented as an outsider, a representative of an attractive but dangerous foreign culture.

Liszt: *A Faust Symphony,* First Movement

The *Faust Symphony* of Liszt is a masterpiece of Romantic program music and a fascinating work to analyze. The three movements represent the three main characters of the Faust legend—Faust, Gretchen, and Mephistopheles. Added to the final movement is an apotheosis, during which a tenor soloist and male chorus sing the last few lines of Goethe's *Faust.*

The most important element in this work is the technique of thematic transformation. All the themes of the long first movement are derived from a few melodic cells or motives; as these basic cells are given different musical shape, they are transformed into distinct themes or leitmotifs that represent the different sides of the hero—mystery, heroism, passion, tender love, and so on. One analytic approach might focus on the cells and the different thematic shape they take on. Another analysis might focus on structure. The first movement is very long and somewhat rambling; the question of underlying structure in a Romantic movement of this size is always an interesting one to pursue. Is the form derived from a program, or is there some intrinsically musical form that guides the organization of this sprawling movement? Another interesting study would be a comparison of the first and third movements, since most of the themes representing Mephistopheles are parodies of the Faust themes. In other words, the melodic cells that are manipulated and transformed in the first movement are further transformed in the final movement to depict completely different ideas and feelings. Other important elements for analysis include the rich harmonic language of late Romanticism and Liszt's effective use of the large orchestral forces.

This work naturally suggests a wide variety of potential topics from the area of cultural studies. Although the Faust legend began in the Renaissance and the best-known version of it, by Goethe, has elements of Enlightenment thinking, we know that this story was a favorite of the Romantic era. There are many musical settings derived from the story; it would be interesting, for example, to compare Liszt's symphony with Mahler's Eighth Symphony, which uses some of the same material from Goethe's *Faust.* The question of characterization in Liszt's work is fascinating. Gretchen is presented in the second movement as innocent and pure, a center of serenity and love in the whirlwind of Faust's endless quest. This is exactly the sort of nineteenth-century depiction of woman—"das ewig Weibliche," woman on a pedestal, a beacon and inspiration for the hero—that feminists justly object to. Another interesting issue is the philosophical statement the music makes about Faust and Mephistopheles. The demon is presented not as a separate being, an external source of evil, but as the dark side of the hero, since Faust's heroic themes from the first movement are mocked and transformed into grotesque cackling in the third. The autobiographical side of the work might be interesting to pursue as well. Liszt was fascinated with the satanic and the grotesque, as seen in compositions such as the *Mephisto Waltz* and *Totentanz;* Faust's redemption through religion and the love of an innocent woman may represent the way Liszt viewed his own life, or the life of any artist. This complex work sometimes puts people off because of its moments of bombast and overreaching, but it illustrates perfectly both the Romantic spirit and the rich possibilities for research, both analytical and cultural, that such works suggest.

Stravinsky: *The Rite of Spring,* Opening Sections

Although *The Rite of Spring* is by now a classic of the early twentieth century, it calls for analytical methods that are different from those appropriate for music of the eighteenth and nineteenth centuries. In this landmark work, Stravinsky rearranged the elements of music and their relative importance to create a style appropriate to the story and the ballet. In this style, rhythm is all-important, melody less so; the few tunes in this section, some borrowed from Russian folk music, are fragmentary, narrow-range motives that repeat obsessively. Ostinato techniques and increasing thickness of texture take the place of traditional development. Instruments are used in new ways; the whole orchestra is sometimes used as a large percussion section. Form is articulated through rhythm and orchestration as much as through melodic material or harmonic cadences. Analysis of this work must begin with an understanding of the succession of musical events rather than with an attempt to find traditional forms. The historical importance of this work comes from the fact that, though its purpose is a nineteenth-century one—it is, after all, program music designed to accompany a ballet—its musical language is in many ways new.

One might focus an analytic study of this work on either the new elements or the traditional aspects of the work. It would also be fruitful to compare it with its immediate predecessors, *Firebird* and *Petrushka,* to isolate the new elements in this work. One might also compare the orchestral score with the version for two pianos that Stravinsky later arranged. In any case, *The Rite of Spring* is certainly a work that demands to be analyzed on its own terms.

There are several obvious nonanalytic research topics suggested by this work. It is generally described as an example of primitivism, an important artistic movement of the early twentieth century. The concept behind primitivism was that European culture had become stodgy and effete; the only way new vitality could be injected into the culture was to borrow ideas from other, more vital cultures. Thus, Picasso and other visual artists turned to African masks for inspiration, and one group of rebel painters christened themselves "Les Fauves" ("The Savages"). The notion that the musics of other cultures, or music from other levels of one's own culture, such as jazz and popular music, should be co-opted in order to breathe new life and vibrancy into "high culture" crops up frequently in the history of Western music and is an fascinating concept to pursue. Another cultural issue is the one of reception. Richard Taruskin, a noted Stravinsky scholar, has written that the premiere of *The Rite of Spring* was not the wild riot that we are used to reading about, and that the catcalls were provoked by the choreography, not the music. Concert performances of the music that took place shortly after the premiere were not marked by civil disorder of any kind. Another area suggested by this work is the connection between dance and music in the twentieth century; as musicians, we sometimes forget that composers as diverse as Debussy, Stravinsky, Copland, and Cage spent much of their careers collaborating with dance companies.

In conclusion, note that these brief comments do not pretend to be exhaustive lists of areas of research that these works suggest. My remarks are intended only as preliminary indications of directions you might take in developing topics for analysis or other kinds of research connected with these pieces. If you plan to do analytical research, note that each work must be studied in ways that illuminate its particular organization. In one sense, stylistic analysis is a circular process. Its goal is the understanding of a musical style, but one cannot begin the analysis until one has enough awareness of the style to be able to choose appropriate methods of analysis. An analysis that asks the wrong questions or searches for the wrong stylistic characteristics will never produce insight into the organization and coherence of a work. At the start of an analytic project, one may need to put aside the specific work for a while and first develop an awareness of the stylistic context from which it came.

Finally, I emphasize again that not every research paper for a class in music must be analytical in design and purpose. The foregoing suggestions about the kinds of nonanalytical research these works suggest do not pretend to be any more exhaustive than the suggestions about analytical directions. My purpose has been to show that any individual piece of music can suggest areas for research, both analytical and cultural, if we brainstorm for a moment. I close this discussion with one last reminder that, whatever direction your research might take, anything you say in a project about music must be based on a solid understanding of the style and organization of the music you are discussing—what holds it together as a unified work of art and what makes it unique.

The next chapter moves into a discussion of the nature of research, some basic resources for research, both print and electronic, and basic research methodologies.

CHAPTER 3

Getting Started: Research

This chapter discusses the first phase of the process of producing a paper on a musical topic—the research phase. Naturally, the process will vary greatly, depending on the topic; each project will call for its own specific resources. In this chapter, we will discuss basic resources and places to start, rather than the resources for highly specialized research. For further information on specialized resources, consult the texts designed for graduate researchers listed in the Preface, especially the Duckles/Reed bibliography and the Wingell/Herzog book. Here we are more concerned with the process of research and how to get started on an undergraduate research project.

CHOOSING A TOPIC

In many undergraduate classes, choosing a topic may not be an issue for the student: The professor may assign a single topic for the whole class. When you do have to choose a topic, however, the following considerations may be helpful.

When the project is first discussed, you need to have a clear idea of the kind of paper the professor has in mind. Pay close attention to the handout explaining the assignment and to the explanation in class so that you clearly understand the professor's expectations and do not waste time dreaming up projects that will not be acceptable. The time to ask questions about the range of acceptable topics is when the assignment is first given, not shortly before the project is due.

Once you understand what sort of topic is expected, you need to choose a general research area and then narrow that area down to a specific topic. One way to begin selecting a topic is to survey the range of genres within the historical period specified by the assignment. If the class covers Baroque music, for example, you might first decide whether you want to work with instrumental or vocal music. If you choose the vocal area, the next step is to select from the various genres—for example, opera, cantata, sacred concerto, or oratorio. If you decide on opera, then you must choose from the various styles—Florentine, Venetian, Neapolitan, French, German, and English. Next, you might want to choose a specific time period, composer, or work. Another way to select a topic is to start with a particular time period or geographical area and find a suitable topic related to that time or place. There are many ways to choose a topic; the important thing is to begin making that decision early, long before the project is due.

During this early stage, you need to do some preliminary browsing in the music library to see what scores and recordings are available and what the secondary literature has to say. "Secondary literature" means reference books, histories, biographies, articles, or anything else published by later generations of scholars, as opposed to "primary sources," the manuscripts, early prints, and similar materials that come from the period you are studying. There is little point in choosing an attractive topic if there are no scores available and nothing has been written about the topic in the secondary sources. If it becomes clear that investigating a topic would involve sending for microfilms of unpublished materials from a European library, spending three months in a European archive, or traveling to some remote corner of the globe to interview a living composer, you probably should choose another topic. If it turns out that you would need to acquire knowledge in new fields, facility in unfamiliar languages, or training in new methodologies to investigate a topic, then that topic clearly does not make sense for a semester or term project.

Once you have decided on a topic, clear your idea with the professor before going much further with your research. Do not waste valuable time working on a topic that may not be acceptable or one that the professor knows will not be suitable for an undergraduate project.

The main goal in choosing a topic is to select something of the right scope. The topic should be specific enough that you can cover it adequately in a paper of normal length, but not so specific that materials are not available or that you have to move into levels of research for which you are not qualified. "The Symphonies of Haydn," for example, is too broad a topic for a term paper. In a paper of fifteen or twenty pages, you might be able to list all the symphonies, their keys and instrumentation, and a fact or two about each, but the result would be a preliminary list, another version of the lists and brief discussions already available in the secondary literature. On the other hand, you are not expected at this stage to solve highly technical research problems such as whether or not an obscure work is actually the work of Haydn; that kind of research problem is better left to experienced scholars. There is a wide range of possibilities between these two extremes. You might choose to compare an early symphony with a later one, determining through comparative analysis how Haydn's style changed over the course of his career. You might focus on a few first movements, comparing different versions of the sonata-allegro process; you might concentrate on the question of structure in a few slow movements. You might compare a symphony by Haydn with one by Mozart, in an attempt to isolate the subtle differences between the two composers. Moving beyond analytical topics, you might focus on performance practice issues or the circumstances in which these works were first performed. You might also concentrate on reception history—that is, how these works were regarded in their time or by later ages. There are hundreds of viable topics within the general area of Haydn symphonies; it takes some thought and some preliminary work with the scores and secondary sources to find a topic that will work for you. Since you will spend considerable time working on the topic you finally settle on, be sure that it is a topic you like, one you are qualified to tackle, and one you can carry through to a successful conclusion.

KINDS OF TOPICS

Most undergraduate research papers fall into a few standard types; as you think about possible topics, it may be helpful to think in terms of these standard types.

One type of topic focuses on analysis of a single work. Assigned topics often fall into this classification; the instructor, knowing that a particular work is an especially fruitful topic for analysis or a useful example of an important style, directs the students to analyze that work and report their conclusions. A paper on a single work typically begins with a review of the background of the work and a summary of what has been written about the work in secondary sources. The main body of the paper would be the student's analysis of the work, followed by a short conclusion and a bibliography.

Another type of topic is a comparative analysis—for example, a comparison of early and late symphonies by Haydn. Analysis of similar works by different composers can be very instructive as well. A project that has worked well in classes on Renaissance music, for example, is a comparison of Dufay's *L'Homme armé* Mass with one of Josquin's Masses on the same cantus firmus. Because the two works utilize the same source material, compositional process, and basic style, the comparison isolates and sheds light on the differences in personal style between the two composers. If you are trying to design a comparative analysis project, it is important that the works be closely related stylistically. A study comparing a Schoenberg twelve-tone piece with a neoclassical work by Stravinsky would no doubt conclude that the two works are fundamentally different—not exactly a world-shaking discovery. On the other hand, it would be interesting to compare twelve-tone works by

Schoenberg and Webern, since that study would presumably uncover individual stylistic differences within the same compositional process.

Sometimes it is useful to survey a larger group of related works in the same style. The danger in dealing with a large body of literature is that the student may end up producing a glorified list, dull to assemble and boring to read. That sort of project is useful only when such surveys do not already exist and the student has some personal reason to produce such a list, such as compiling a graded and annotated repertory of pieces for teaching purposes.

Finally, there are biographical and historical studies that do not focus on analysis of specific works. Such projects might study, for example, a Renaissance court and its musical life, or the musical situation in turn-of-the-century Vienna. A biographical study of an important performer of the Baroque era, such as the castrato Farinelli or Gottfried Reiche, Bach's trumpeter at Leipzig, might shed light on the question of the importance of performers to the evolution of musical style, as well as the ways in which musical careers in that era differed from careers now. There are some potential problems connected with historical, biographical, or sociological topics. First, topics of this sort can sometimes result in summaries of material already available in standard sources, in which case they are largely pointless busywork. Any research paper must have something new to offer—if not new information, then an original thesis, a fresh approach, or a thought-provoking conclusion. Second, students sometimes propose topics that are too broad, either because of the large repertory of works they wish to cover or because of the combination of disciplines and research skills needed to do the sort of work they propose. In choosing a topic, it is good to be curious and adventurous; it is also good to be practical and choose topics that are within your competence to complete in the assigned time period.

You can now understand why professors sometimes assign specific topics, require students to choose from a prepared list of topics, or insist on approving topics early in the semester. Some topics work, some do not, and some would take years to cover adequately. Trust your professor's judgment about topics; if you are intent on pursuing an unusual topic, most instructors will try to help you pursue that interest and still produce a successful paper.

WHAT RESEARCH MEANS

Once you have a workable topic, the next step is to investigate that topic through the process called research. It is important to understand that research is more than just locating a group of relevant quotations and stringing them together in a paper, even assuming that the writer includes quotation marks and appropriate footnotes. Reporting what authorities have said about a topic may be a useful way to begin a paper, but it does not fulfill the researcher's responsibility. Research in any field must have a creative, per-

sonal side, especially in the arts, where we study the products of human freedom and artistic vision. Even research in the natural sciences involves more
than merely measuring and quantifying phenomena. It takes a creative
mind to make the leap necessary to create a hypothesis that can explain puzzling phenomena and the correct means to test that hypothesis. Research in
the arts is not just gathering information, any more than musical analysis
consists of listing and quantifying musical events. Facts by themselves are
useless unless they lead to ideas. One must have a thesis and a conclusion;
a paper that includes a detailed review of the literature but does not then
move to the writer's own ideas is a book report, not a research project.

At some point as you are gathering information, all your observations
and thoughts should begin to coalesce around one central point, the main
thesis of your paper. The reader wants to know what you think. Do you agree
with the secondary sources? Does your analysis of the music, or the other
kinds of research you have done, lead you to side with one opinion rather
than the others or to disagree with them all? Does your view of the work dif-
fer from the view reported in the standard literature?

Your hypothesis and conclusion need not be world-shaking. The reader
of undergraduate papers does not expect to see conclusions like "This cantata could not possibly have been written by Bach," or "The Mendelssohn
Violin Concerto is actually based on a twelve-tone row." The reader does expect, however, to see your informed opinion, based on the research you
have done. Too many papers stop abruptly after reporting on the secondary
literature and the analysis process, as if the last few pages of the project were
missing. As a scholar and a musician, even if you regard yourself as an ap-
prentice in one or both fields, you have a responsibility to follow the research process to its conclusion, to risk taking a position, and to communicate your informed ideas and opinions about your topic.

GATHERING MATERIALS

Once you have a workable topic and approach, the next step is to gather the
materials you need. Start by assembling a bibliography on the topic. It is crucial that you be thorough and systematic right from the beginning of your
search. Set aside a large block of time for this step, take careful notes on what
you find, and keep your information in some organized fashion—in a file on
your computer, in a notebook or folder, or on note cards. Whatever system
you use for gathering and storing information, it is important to be thorough, consistent, and systematic. There is nothing worse than discovering
at the last minute, when the deadline is pressing, that your notes are incomplete or no longer make sense to you. Each entry should include complete bibliographic information so that you do not have to return to each
book to find the date of publication, the page on which the material you

want to quote appears, and other such details. The more complete and consistent your note-taking system is, the easier it will be to use the material when you get to the writing stage.

PLACES TO START: PRINT RESOURCES

As you begin the search for information on your topic, start with the standard kinds of resources. The first thing to be aware of is that bibliographies on many topics have already been assembled and are published in several places. Rather than reinventing the wheel, start with these existing bibliographies; you will not only save considerable time and effort but also be much less likely to overlook important sources. Extensive lists of published bibliographies appear in the guides for graduate students; here are some basic resources, with some advice on how to use them.

Library Catalogs

The first place to begin your search for information is the catalog of a good music library. The next section will deal with on-line catalogs; here we are concerned with printed resources. Library catalogs have standard ways of dividing topics into large headings and subtopics; a new researcher should spend some time browsing through a card catalog (if your library still has one) to get a sense of these patterns and the standard subheadings they use. In addition, all library catalogs use the same official system for dealing with such matters as spelling and alphabetizing composers' names and transliterating the names of composers from foreign alphabets. The more experience you have with the way catalogs work, the easier it will be to find what you are looking for. Be patient and resourceful; you may not find what you are looking for in the first place you look. Never give up quickly; look for cross-references, try a different spelling or a different key word; start from the name of an author who you know has written about the subject; or design some other path to find what you are looking for.

Dictionaries and Encyclopedias

Another good strategy in the early stages of a research project is to consult music dictionaries and encyclopedias. The following are some of the standard musical reference works.

Single-Volume References

Baker's Biographical Dictionary of Musicians. 8th ed. Edited by Nicolas Slonimsky. New York: Schirmer, 1991.
Harvard Biographical Dictionary of Music. Edited by Don Michael Randel. Cambridge: Harvard University Press, 1996.

The New Harvard Dictionary of Music. Edited by Don Michael Randel. Cambridge: Belknap Press of Harvard University Press, 1986.

Multivolume References

Die Musik in Geschichte und Gegenwart. Edited by Friedrich Blume. Kassel: Bärenreiter, 1949–1979; 2nd ed., 1994–.
The New Grove Dictionary of Music and Musicians. 2nd ed. Edited by Stanley Sadie and John Tyrell. London: Macmillan, 2001.

A word about the three single-volume dictionaries first. The first two, *Baker's Biographical Dictionary* and the *Harvard Biographical Dictionary,* are one-volume biographical dictionaries; that is, they contain entries on composers, performers, and theorists and include worklists and selective bibliographies. These dictionaries do not, of course, have entries for instruments, terms, genres, or periods. *The New Harvard Dictionary of Music,* a complete revision of an earlier work edited by Willi Apel, is a one-volume dictionary of terms, with some longer articles and useful selective bibliographies. Many researchers keep the *New Harvard Dictionary* and one of the biographical dictionaries in their personal libraries for handy reference.

The *New Grove,* as it is familiarly called, is the most important encyclopedia of music, since it contains the most up-to-date information, worklists, and bibliographies. It is obviously the best place to start looking for bibliographical information. The first edition of the *New Grove* was published in twenty volumes in 1980; you have probably seen copies of the first edition in music libraries, by now somewhat the worse for wear after two decades of heavy use. The second edition, which appeared on library shelves in March 2001, has twenty-nine volumes, including an index volume. Each article was written by an expert in that particular field; some articles are the length of a monograph or a small book, and all contain complete worklists and bibliographies that were up-to-date at the time of publication. All music libraries have this basic resource on their reference shelves; it can be found in many public libraries as well. Always check the *New Grove* when you are starting on a project, and use some imagination as you search for information; the material you seek might be found in an article on the composer or in articles on genres, instruments, terms, or historical eras. The second edition is available on line as well as in print; we will have more to say about that in the section on electronic resources.

Die Musik in Geschichte und Gegenwart, known familiarly as MGG, is the most important German music lexicon. A second edition of this work began to appear in 1994; it is divided into nine volumes of information organized by subject, all of which have been published, and further volumes of biographical entries, which are still being published at the time of this writing. The MGG is particularly valuable for its coverage of German topics and world music, as well as for its copious illustrations.

There are other dictionaries in the *New Grove* series, supplementary works that deal with specialized areas; obviously, these are the best places to start research for topics in those areas. Some of the material in these supplementary lexicons is taken directly from the main dictionary; some is new.

The New Grove Dictionary of American Music. 4 vols. Edited by Stanley Sadie and
 H. Wiley Hitchcock. New York: Grove Dictionaries, 1986.
The New Grove Dictionary of Jazz. 2 vols. Edited by Barry Kernfeld. New York: Grove
 Dictionaries, 1988.
The New Grove Dictionary of Musical Instruments. 3 vols. Edited by Stanley Sadie. Lon-
 don: Macmillan, 1980.
The New Grove Dictionary of Opera. 4 vols. Edited by Stanley Sadie. New York: Grove
 Dictionaries, 1992.

There are many other dictionaries of music; the handful listed above are the main sources for most topics. One issue to consider in using these resources is how to locate the most up-to-date bibliographical listings, since any published bibliography is at least slightly out of date by the time it is published; such resources are constantly being revised and updated. As I prepare this revision for publication, the *New Grove* is the most recently published of the large encyclopedias. However, since MGG is still in the process of publishing its second edition, a year or two from now the most up-to-date bibliographical information on some topics might be found not in the *New Grove,* at least not in the print version, but in MGG.

Histories of Music

Most histories of music include bibliographical notes, located either at the end of each chapter or at the back of the book. These bibliographies are another good place to start, once you locate the appropriate chapter in the book or series that deals with the area you are researching. The following are the standard one-volume histories.

Crocker, Richard L. *A History of Musical Style.* New York: McGraw-Hill, 1966. Reprint,
 New York: Dover, 1986. The bibliography, entitled "Selected Study Materials"
 and organized by chapters, begins on page 538.
Grout, Donald J., and Claude V. Palisca. *A History of Western Music.* 6th ed. New
 York: W. W. Norton & Co., 2001. Bibliographies appear at the end of each
 chapter.
Rosenstiel, Leonie, general editor. *Schirmer History of Music.* New York: Schirmer,
 1982. Bibliographies appear at the end of each chapter.
Stolba, K. Marie. *The Development of Western Music: A History.* 2nd ed. Madison, WI:
 Brown and Benchmark, 1994. The bibliography, organized by chapters, ap-
 pears at the end of the book.

The multivolume histories of music also contain useful selective bibliographies. Among the standard music history series are the following publications.

The New Oxford History of Music. London, New York: Oxford, 1954–90. Each of ten volumes covers a different period and is a collection of essays by different writers, rather than a continuous narrative. The first two volumes have been published in extensively revised second editions.

Norton Introduction to Music History Series. New York: Norton, 1978–. Intended to supplement the older History of Music Series. Each volume has a companion anthology of scores. Extensive bibliographies, organized by chapter, appear at the back of each volume in the series. At the time of writing, the publisher indicates that the Baroque volume is forthcoming.

Hoppin, Richard. *Medieval Music.* 1978.
Atlas, Alan. *Renaissance Music.* 1998.
Downs, Philip G. *Classical Music.* 1992.
Plantinga, Leon. *Romantic Music.* 1984.
Morgan, Robert P. *Twentieth-Century Music.* 1990.

The Prentice Hall History of Music Series. Upper Saddle River, NJ: Prentice Hall, 1965–. The first six volumes listed focus on the various periods of Western music; there are also several volumes on American music and world musics. Bibliographical notes appear at the conclusion of each chapter. Some volumes are out of print but are still available in libraries.

Yudkin, Jeremy. *Music in Medieval Europe.* 1989. Replaced Albert Seay, *Music in the Medieval World,* 1965; 2nd ed., 1975.
Brown, Howard Mayer, and Louise K. Stein. *Music in the Renaissance.* 2nd ed., 1999.
Palisca, Claude V. *Baroque Music.* 3rd ed., 1991.
Pauly, Reinhard G. *Music in the Classic Period.* 4th ed., 2000.
Longyear, Rey M. *Nineteenth-Century Romanticism in Music.* 3rd ed., 1988.
Salzman, Eric. *Twentieth-Century Music: An Introduction.* 4th ed., 2002.
Nettl, Bruno. *Folk and Traditional Music of the Western Continents.* 3rd ed., revised and edited by Valerie Woodring Goertzen, 1990.
Malm, William P. *Music Cultures of the Pacific, the Near East, and Asia.* 3rd ed., 1996.
Hitchcock, H. Wiley. *Music in the United States: A Historical Introduction.* 4th ed., 2000. The final chapter was contributed by Kyle Gann.
Béhague, Gérard. *Music in Latin America: An Introduction.* 1979.

Music and Society Series. A series of eight books, edited by Stanley Sadie and published by Prentice Hall, designed to present music "in a broad context of socio-political, economic, intellectual, and religious life." Each volume is a collection of articles on a particular historical era by various authors. The first two volumes to appear, on the Renaissance and the Classical eras, were published under the series title "Man and Music"; the other eight were published as the "Music and Society" Series. Unfortunately, at this writing many of these useful volumes are out of print; they still may be found in music libraries.

James McKinnon, ed. *Antiquity and the Middle Ages: From Ancient Greece to the 15th Century.* 1991.
Fenlon, Iain, ed. *The Renaissance: From the 1470s to the End of the 16th Century.* 1989.
Price, Curtis, ed. *The Early Baroque Era: From the Late 16th Century to the 1660s.* 1994.
Buelow, George, ed. *The Late Baroque Era: From the 1680s to 1740.* 1994.

Zaslaw, Neal, ed. *The Classical Era: From the 1740s to the End of the 18th Century.* 1989.
Ringer, Alexander, ed. *The Early Romantic Era: Between Revolutions, 1789 and 1848.* 1991.
Samson, Jim, ed. *The Late Romantic Era: From the Mid-19th Century to World War I.* 1991.
Morgan, Robert, ed. *Modern Times: From World War I to the Present.* 1994.

Biographies

If there is a published biography of the composer you are studying, it may be very helpful for your project, particularly if it is a "life and works," including description and analysis of the composer's works. Biographies are classified in the Library of Congress system under the number ML [for Music Literature] 410; within that section, books are shelved alphabetically by composer, so that one browses for biographies by looking under the composer's name. In the Dewey Decimal System, all biographies are shelved together under the classification 92 (shorthand for 920), then alphabetically by subject; thus, biographies of composers are located with all the other biographies. Not all biographies of composers and performers are serious research studies; later in this chapter, we will discuss the researcher's responsibility to evaluate sources and use them carefully. Still, biographies can be an important resource for research.

Thematic Catalogs

If a composer's works have been listed in a thematic catalog (the German term is *Verzeichnis*), the researcher may find such a catalog very helpful. The most famous examples of thematic catalogs are Schmieder's *Bach-Werke-Verzeichnis*, which is organized by genre, and the Köchel catalog of the works of Mozart, organized chronologically. These are only the best-known examples; a random sampling of composers whose works have been systematically cataloged includes composers as diverse as Beethoven, Brahms, Busoni, Clementi, Haydn, Lully, Schubert, Schoenberg, Shostakovich, Strauss, Stravinsky, Vivaldi, Wagner, and Walton. A complete list of thematic catalogs may be found in Barry S. Brook, *Thematic Catalogues in Music: An Annotated Bibliography* (Hillsdale, NY: Pendragon Press, 1972; rev. ed., 1977). Catalogs published after that date are indexed in *The International Inventory of Music Literature.* (See the discussion of this important resource in the following section.) One advantage of using these resources is that the entry for each work includes not only information on the background of the work, surviving manuscripts, early editions, and so forth, but also a bibliography on that specific work. In the Bach catalog, for instance, the entry for each cantata lists articles on that particular cantata as well as the pages in general books where that work is discussed. The efficient researcher will want to take advantage of these resources.

Articles

An enormous body of recent research has not yet found its way into the standard histories and is available only in musicological journals, such as *The Journal of the American Musicological Society, The Journal of Musicology, Musical Quarterly, Acta Musicologica,* and *Music Review.* Articles are the only source of substantial information on some topics—the standard one-volume histories can hardly stay abreast of recent research on all subjects. The best way to acquaint yourself with the journals and get some idea of the sort of research they publish is to browse through the current issues of periodicals in the music library.

Locating articles among the scores of scholarly journals may seem to neophyte researchers to be an intimidating task, but there are resources designed to help them locate articles on specific topics. Many journals publish cumulative listings of the articles they have published. There are also two general guides that list articles published in the musical journals. The first is the *Music Index,* a collection of abstracts of articles published in selected music periodicals. The *Music Index* began publication in 1949; it is published monthly, and cumulative listings are published annually. The quickest way to locate articles in the print version is to search first through the annual cumulative listings and then consult the monthly issues for the abstracts of the articles that look promising. It takes time to go through all the annual listings, but it is an excellent way to locate articles related to your topic.

Another important resource is the *International Inventory of Music Literature,* known as RILM from the initials of its title in French. This index contains abstracts of articles, dissertations, and other publications, and is published several times a year. Cumulative listings are published every five years. Using RILM can save considerable time because of the inclusiveness of its coverage. Articles in collections that are not regularly indexed or included in card catalogs are indexed in RILM; it can be very helpful indeed. Both *Music Index* and RILM are now available in searchable formats besides the print versions; see the section on electronic resources.

Dissertations

Doctoral dissertations can be very helpful to the researcher, since they are typically based on primary resources and include complete bibliographies. Reference libraries contain published lists of dissertations accepted in American and European libraries and abstracts of dissertations published by University Microfilms of Ann Arbor. Music libraries frequently order copies of dissertations, and anyone can order a copy of a dissertation from University Microfilms. If you find a listing of a dissertation you would like to consult but are worried about the cost or about getting a copy in time, talk to your professor; he or she might want to request that the library order a copy.

Titles and abstracts of dissertations are now available also in electronic formats; see the section on electronic resources.

Scores and Recordings

Researchers need to be aware that there are different kinds of scores, some more reliable than others for scholarly research. Primary sources, such as manuscripts and first editions, are the most reliable but the most scarce, and may be difficult for a nonspecialist to locate or read. Scholarly editions constitute the next level; they attempt to present a version of the music that represents as exactly as possible what the composer actually wrote, based on surviving autograph materials and the earliest surviving manuscript and printed editions. Then there are performing scores, some of them quite reliable and others heavily edited. The question of editions is critical with early music. For example, the old performing editions of Bach's keyboard works, edited by Busoni and others, are cluttered with fingerings, slurs, dynamic markings, and other editorial additions that have little to do with what Bach actually wrote. Useful as these markings might be for a young student first learning the piece, scholarly work should be based not on these heavily edited versions but on a clean scholarly edition that tries to duplicate what the composer wrote. It is usually better to find a reliable scholarly edition in the collected sets or collected works of a composer and make a photocopy of that score to use as your working copy than it is to base your work on a more accessible performing edition that may or may not faithfully represent what the composer wrote. Collected sets are given M2 and M3 numbers, and shelved in the library's noncirculating score section. The collections in the M2 section are organized by countries or genres; the M3 section contains the collected works of individual composers, organized alphabetically by composer's last name. Browse through the M2 and M3 sections of your music library to get some sense of the wealth of scholarly editions available to you. The Dewey Decimal System groups these editions similarly and has special numbers for each type of collection. There are three published guides to collected sets; they are found in the reference sections of most music libraries.

Charles, Sydney Robinson. *A Handbook of Music and Music Literature in Sets and Series.* New York: Free Press; London: Collier-Macmillan, 1972.
Heyer, Anna, comp. *Historical Sets, Collected Editions, and Monuments of Music,* 3rd ed. 2 vols. Chicago: American Library Assoc., 1980.
Hill, George R., and Norris L. Stephens. *Collected Editions, Historical Sets, and Monuments of Music.* Berkeley, CA: Fallen Leaf Press, 1997.

Recordings may be part of your research for a project; the same critical judgment must be applied to recordings as to scores, perhaps especially in the case of music before 1900. Although we know more about historically informed performance practice than we did some years ago, many questions are still hotly contested issues, and we have no final answers. Still, if you have a choice of recordings to use for your project, it makes sense to choose one that takes historical authenticity as one of its goals. Check the CD booklet to see whether historical instruments were used and how the edition was chosen.

Critical judgment should be applied not only to the recorded performance but also to the accompanying notes. Sometimes these notes are written by well-known experts and based on scholarly research. At other times, the space is devoted instead to biographies of the performers or advertisements for other recordings, with a paragraph or two left for discussion of the music. Serious notes, especially those signed by a known expert, or booklets included with multi-CD sets, are certainly appropriate to cite in a paper. Brief, unsigned comments, on the other hand, are not likely to provide the sort of material that you would want to cite.

PLACES TO START: ELECTRONIC RESOURCES

As you are well aware, there has been a revolution in the last ten or twenty years in the way information is stored and transmitted. The personal computer now stands alongside the library as a sophisticated tool for research; information now circulates on disks and Web sites as well as on pieces of paper. The Internet is clearly established as the primary electronic locus for storing and disseminating information; it has expanded so rapidly and contains such a dizzying number and variety of sites that now there is talk of a new network, Internet II, that universities are building for serious research. There is a detailed discussion of electronic resources for research in Chapter 4 of *Introduction to Research in Music,* the graduate text cited in the Preface; here we will discuss some of the main types of electronic resources that are useful for research and some hints about using them.

On-line Library Catalogs

Most libraries now provide access to their catalogs on line; when you walk into any library, even local branches of the public library, the first thing you see is a bank of workstations with computers for searching the library's holdings. Some libraries still keep their card catalogs as well; in other libraries, the electronic catalog is now the only catalog, or at least the only one that is up-to-date and available to the user. As you probably are aware, in-house library catalogs are user-friendly and efficient, provided that the researcher has a basic understanding of how these catalogs work. Most on-line library catalogs have clear on-screen commands; one can generally walk into a library for the first time and use that library's system with no difficulty. You must remember, however, that computers are very literal; they do only what we ask them to do, not what we mean to ask. You may not get any response to the first title, name, or search word you enter. You may have to try alternative spellings of the names of composers or works, try different key words, or design other circuitous paths to reach the information you seek. There is little point in trying to discuss the peculiarities of on-line catalogs; experience and practice with the system at your library will acquaint you with the strategies that work best on that particular system. The important thing to realize is that a negative result on your opening move is just the start of the game and should not discourage you from attempting to find other ways to coax the information from the system.

Many on-line library catalogs also provide access to the catalogs of other libraries, perhaps larger music libraries in your area, as well as listings from research libraries elsewhere in the United States and the world. In addition, library catalogs are usually available somewhere on your school's Web sites, so that you can do bibliographic searches of your own library and other important libraries around the country and the world from your own room and on your own schedule. Take the time to learn how to navigate around these valuable resources.

Databases on CD-ROM

As I mentioned in the section on print resources, some databases of bibliographic information are published in both print and CD-ROM formats. The advantages of searching a database on CD-ROM over the print version should be obvious; a CD-ROM can hold a large amount of information that is searchable, like an on-line library catalog, by using names of authors, subjects, or key words. It is also easier to search through a single disc than to shuffle through a shelf of annual indexes and monthly volumes of abstracts in the print versions. Note that annual updated versions of the databases on CD-ROM are made available to libraries by subscription, which means that the researcher has to sit in the library to use these resources and is, therefore, limited by library hours and availability of computer workstations.

The most important databases available in CD-ROM format are the *Music Index,* which contains abstracts of articles published in a wide variety of periodicals on music; *International Index to Music Periodicals* (IIMP), which indexes articles in 370 music journals; RILM, a collection of abstracts of articles in periodicals and collections, dissertations, and some books; and *Dissertations Abstracts,* which lists titles and abstracts for dissertations and theses. Most college and university music libraries should have these CDs. As is the case with on-line catalogs, each of these resources has its own peculiarities, and you need to be imaginative and resourceful to design alternative search strategies if your first attempt does not succeed. Note that some of these databases are also available on the Internet, provided that your school subscribes to the service and can provide you with the necessary password.

It seems clear that the databases that are available on the Internet—at this writing, IIMP and RILM—will cease publishing the versions on CD-ROM. On the other hand, at this writing, *Music Index* is not available on the Internet, and therefore researchers should be aware of the resources available on CD-ROM and how to use them.

The Internet

The Internet has gradually taken over as the resource of choice for storing and retrieving information. Many organizations that first used the Telnet system for information storage and retrieval have moved their sites to the Internet; sites on the latter system are more visually appealing and more easily navigable—"user-friendly," as we say—than sites on the older Telnet system. The Internet, as you are aware, is not a perfect information source; sometimes the information superhighway feels more like a congested freeway at rush hour. Some students live half their lives on the Web, e-mailing friends, downloading tunes, playing games, and surfing through the colorful and seductive electronic world. The glory of the Web is also its main problem; anyone can put anything on a Web site, and there are Web sites to serve every conceivable human interest and advertise every imaginable kind of product or service. You can sit in your room and check out places to stay in London, Paris, or Vienna, order opera tickets from any opera house in the world, scan huge files of information on your favorite film or TV show, buy a car, take a course, choose a college to attend, look at homes to purchase, do your banking, buy books and CDs, order clothes, even purchase an illegal term paper. A recent article on college life maintained that some students have become so fond of the ethernet connections in their campus housing that they are reluctant to go home for vacations, because at home they have to rely on intolerably slow modems.

This is not the place, however, for a discussion of the Internet's impact on society; we are concerned here with its usefulness for research. First, you should be aware that a vast amount of useful general reference material is available on line; one can find dictionaries of all sorts, encyclopedias of every level, biblical texts and concordances, almanacs, and other general reference resources. There is also a wealth of material useful for research in music. We have already mentioned that the catalogs of your library and many libraries around the country and the world are available on the Internet. Databases such as RILM and *Dissertation Abstracts* are available on the Internet as well, as long as your library subscribes and can provide the necessary password. In this book we cannot list the hundreds of Web sites that might be useful for research on musical topics; we can, however, discuss the kinds of Web sites researchers should be aware of.

We have already mentioned sites that are primarily bibliographical. This category includes the on-line catalogs of libraries and archives; indexes to periodical articles, such as IIMP and RILM; and *Doctoral Dissertations in Musicology On-line*. Music dictionaries and encyclopedias are now available on line; the most exciting new development in musicological research is that the second edition of the *New Grove* is now available on line. One can either take out an annual subscription or pay a nominal fee for the privilege of downloading articles for a limited period of time. The availability of this important resource on line will greatly change the way we do our research. There are also journals that are published only on line and not in print, such as *The Journal of Seventeenth-Century Music*. Publishing on line is particularly appropriate for journals on music; musical examples in an on-line article can include not only excerpts from printed scores but audio files as well. There are also sites that provide information on all conceivable specialized areas within music—choral music, individual composers, individual instruments of all kinds, computers and music, early music, music education, world music, jazz, opera, women in music, and any other topic you can imagine.

The only way to get an idea of what is available on the Internet for music researchers is to spend some time in serious browsing. You can try using a search engine to pursue musical topics, but you will probably find that you uncover mostly commercial sites—companies selling books or recordings. A better way is to explore link sites—collections of sites useful for music students and scholars compiled by schools or organizations. Below are listed a few link sites with their URLs so that you can browse through their long lists of specialized sites that may be useful for your research. Try these sites and click on the links that lead to topics of interest to you; I think you will be amazed at the vast number and variety of these sites.

The American Musicological Society: WWW Sites of Interest to Musicologists. <http://musdra.ucdavis.edu/Documents/AMS/musicology_www.html>.
Society for Music Theory: Links to SMT Online Resources. <http://boethius .music.ucsb. Edu/smt-list/homepage/online-resources.html>.
College Music Society: Music, Arts, and Education Links Page. <http://www .music.org/links.html>.
Indiana University Library: Internet Resources for Music Scholars. <http://www .music.indiana.edu/music_resources/>.
Harvard University Library: Internet Resources for Music Scholars. <http://www .rism.harvard.edu/MusicLibrary/InternetResources.html>.

It is just as important to be systematic and thorough in your research on the Internet as it is in other types of research. When you are working at home, it is easy to bookmark sites you will want to revisit; if you are working in a computer room on campus, you have to write down the URLs of useful sites so that you can return to them. You should also keep a record of all the appropriate information—author, organization, URL, and so on, the equivalent of publication information for books and articles—in case you want to cite the Web site in your footnotes and bibliography.

EVALUATING RESOURCES

It is important for researchers to realize that they must exercise critical judgment when consulting published materials of any sort. Not everything you find in print or on the Internet is to be taken as gospel truth or followed blindly. Not all biographies, for example, are scholarly studies. Biographies run the gamut from serious studies, such as Robbins Landon's multivolume study of Haydn's life and works, to overromanticized nineteenth-century biographies, which may be entertaining but are not very helpful for scholarly work. If you have to choose between two biographies, the more recent one or the one that shows evidence of serious scholarly research is generally more to be trusted than the earlier or more popular treatment. You know what serious scholarship looks like; books published for the scholarly community come equipped with footnotes, a bibliography, and an index. In addition, they should take account of recent research and should be free of any bias that would cause you to question their reliability. Learn to trust your own judgment; reading a few pages will give you a fair idea of how serious and reliable a book is. Evaluate other kinds of print resources the same way; there are different kinds of journals, different sorts of histories, even different levels of reference works intended for different audiences, and you can quickly tell which resources are intended for serious research and which are not.

Critical judgment is even more necessary when one is doing research on the Internet. Some Web sites are nothing more than the ramblings of enthusiastic individuals with time on their hands, who think their thoughts are of interest to kindred spirits. Such sites are of no more use to research than are the casual remarks made in chat rooms. Many other sites are commercial; sites such as Amazon.com or the companies that sell classical CDs may contain descriptions of books or recordings, but such blurbs are different from the reviews found in scholarly journals. On the other hand, there are scholarly sites that are perfectly appropriate for serious research. The on-line journals, for instance, are refereed just like print journals; that is, articles are accepted for publication only after being read by experts in the field. The difference between scholarly sites and the other sites is as immediately obvious as the difference between serious books and popular fiction, or between *The Journal of the American Musicological Society* and *People* magazine. It is always the researcher's responsibility to treat information critically, no matter where it comes from, and to accept only those sources that seem trustworthy.

Researchers often find that information, right or wrong, is repeated unchallenged from secondary source to secondary source. You are free to take issue with ideas and conclusions found in print; in fact, you must take issue if your research indicates that those ideas are not borne out by the facts or by a careful reading of the evidence. That is precisely what the researcher's task is—to raise questions about what is written in secondary sources. Sources are not to be followed blindly but should be judged realistically and critically. A one-volume history of music, for example, cannot be expected to include up-to-date reports of research findings on every detailed question or the latest information about every composer mentioned; that is not its purpose. On the other hand, you cannot expect a narrowly focused scholarly article to provide the broad view that you would find in a history. Evaluation of sources, both print and electronic, is one of the major responsibilities of the researcher.

FOREIGN-LANGUAGE SOURCES

The responsible researcher cannot ignore important books and articles just because they happen to be written in a language other than English. It is a fact of scholarly life that many important books and articles are written in German, French, Italian, and other languages. German, French, and English are the standard languages in which research is published. German is especially important for most research on musical topics, because the discipline of musicology—*Musikwissenschaft* in German—was first developed in German universities, and many scholarly resources are still published in German. If you do not read German, and it becomes clear that a book or article in German is a crucial source for your topic, ask someone who knows German to translate the relevant sections for you. There are people on college campuses, both faculty and students, who can read any language under the sun. Bear in mind, also, that tables and bibliographies are exactly the same in German sources as in English ones. Students sometimes avoid using the Schmieder catalog of Bach's works, for instance, because "it's in German," when the bibliographies are exactly the same as they would be in English. The book can be useful to anyone, regardless of language experience.

WHEN TO STOP: HOW MUCH RESEARCH IS ENOUGH?

The point at which you decide that you have gathered enough information for a paper will vary, depending on the topic and the limits set by the instructor when the paper was assigned. Students understand that the bibliography for an undergraduate project is not expected to have the same length and depth as a bibliography for a graduate paper or thesis, but it is still difficult sometimes to know when to call a halt to the research stage and move on.

There are two extremes to be avoided. Some students are satisfied with a citation or two from their music history textbooks or some nontechnical, all-purpose encyclopedia. In other words, some students gather their information from the wrong kinds of resources and never approach serious research. Others, even though their files are already bulging with citations, keep uncovering new resources that they feel obliged to include. If the research phase seems to be getting out of control, especially if the information you find seems not to support your preliminary hypothesis, it may be time to arrange a conference with your instructor. It may be necessary to negotiate some limits on your research, or you may be approaching your research in the wrong way. It is also possible that your topic is too broad and needs some rethinking. It is probably helpful at that point to step back a bit from your research to see it in perspective and to decide whether what you have done is appropriate for the project.

Near the end of the research phase, all the information should begin to fall into place in your mind, leading to clear ideas and opinions, and coalescing into a logical framework. You must shape this mass of information into a coherent plan. In the interests of unity and coherence, you may not be able to use every item you have uncovered in your research; one always does more research than one can actually include in the paper. The next step is to organize everything you have discovered in the research phase into a logical outline with one central idea or hypothesis, arguments in support of that central idea gathered from secondary sources and from your analysis of the materials, and a conclusion. Thoughtful and diligent research is critical, but it is only the first phase. A mass of information is not a paper; it is only raw material that must be organized into a clear and coherent presentation.

CHAPTER 4

Writing a Research Paper

This chapter describes the process of writing a research paper, step-by-step, after the research phase is completed. Naturally, the writing process will vary, depending on the topic, thesis, and focus of the paper; this chapter will discuss general principles and practical advice applicable to most papers. I assume in this discussion that all students use either personal computers or the equipment in the school computer room to write their papers. Each section will include advice on using a computer in that particular phase of the writing process.

THE OUTLINE

The first step in writing a paper is to design a clear outline, so that when you begin to write, you will know exactly where you are going, what comes next, and which material belongs where. This is the point at which you must make the difficult decisions about what to include, what to leave out, and how to order the material. The outlining stage is crucial and has at least as much impact on the quality of the eventual paper as any other step. It is in the process of outlining that you settle the critical questions of unity, coherence, and logical flow. If your outline is clear and logical, writing the paper will be a matter of putting flesh on the outline's skeleton. If your outline is a jumble of unrelated ideas, your paper is not likely to be clear and convincing.

Topic and Thesis

Every research paper must have a thesis—a topic sentence that represents the point of the paper, the statement the writer wishes to make about the topic, the central, controlling idea of the entire paper. A topic is an area of study; a thesis is the position you take on the topic. "Stravinsky's neoclassi-cism" is a topic; "Stravinsky's *Octet for Winds* is a perfect example of the aes-thetic aims of neoclassicism" is a thesis. The difference between topic and the-sis should be obvious: The topic is general, the thesis is narrow and focused. The thesis is the central statement that represents the writer's creative think-ing about the topic and controls everything else that appears in the paper. The thesis is crucial, because every sentence in the paper must relate to it; the the-sis determines what should be included and what must be left out of the paper. You may start your research with a thesis in mind, or, more likely, the thesis will emerge from your research, as study of the secondary literature and your own discoveries and insights begin to coalesce around a particular idea or position that becomes your personal statement about the topic. As you move from research into the writing process, the first and most important thing you need is a viable thesis that you are enthusiastic about. In a typical paper, an introductory section acquaints the reader with the topic and states the thesis; the rest of the paper presents arguments that support the thesis.

Introduction

The function of an introduction is to ease into your topic, put it in some perspective, and announce the thesis of your paper. Browse through some articles in the musicological journals to see how introductions work. They often start with a general idea and then move to the specific topic and thesis of the paper; it is also possible to move in the other direction, starting with a specific fact or event and progressing to a broader issue.

There are two extremes to be avoided in introductions. One is to skip the introduction altogether or write only a sentence or two, creating an abrupt opening that plunges directly into the body of the paper, disorient-ing the reader. Suppose a paper began like this: "In the first measure of this violin concerto, we can already see the ideas that Bach used as the basis for the entire movement." The reader thinks, "Wait a minute—what are we talk-ing about? Which period? Which Bach—J. S., C. P. E., J. C., or P. D. Q.? Which work? Which movement?" The fact that the paper has a title that an-nounces the topic does not free the writer from the obligation to lead the reader into the topic once the paper begins. An introduction should intro-duce the general topic, the specific area the paper will deal with, and the the-sis that the paper will argue.

The other extreme is to write a long introduction that develops a life of its own and becomes a separate paper, bringing up issues that are not germane to the main point of the paper and meandering away from the topic instead of leading the reader into it. Books on writing recommend as a general rule that an introduction occupy no more than one-tenth of the paper's length. Some-times a paper requires a longer introduction; for example, it may be necessary to define complex terms and concepts or explain some important background material. Generally, if the introduction to a paper of fifteen pages runs beyond two or three pages, the writer needs to hunt down and delete the extraneous material.

The introduction should include a clear idea of where the paper is going and announce the thesis that you will defend. At the outline stage, decide exactly how you will introduce your topic and thesis, and what you plan to include in your introduction.

Body

Next, outline the main points of the body of your paper, including all the subtopics that will be included in each of the main points. It is a good idea to work out your outline in considerable detail, even to the level of individual paragraphs, so that when you begin writing you know exactly what goes where and what comes next. It is at this point that you must decide the order in which the material will be presented. You should also include in your outline some idea of the methodology to be followed in establishing each point—where you will use quotations from the secondary sources, where musical examples will be most effective, which points depend on analysis, and so forth. You should end with an outline so specific that if you were to submit the outline alone, your instructor would have a clear idea of what you intend to accomplish in your paper. The more time you spend fussing with the outline, the more logical, coherent, and convincing your paper will be.

Conclusion

Often the most difficult section of a paper to write is the conclusion. At this point, the writer often feels that there is nothing left to say. Conclusions are necessary, however, not only to reemphasize the main point, but also to wrap up the study in a tidy, memorable way. You can connect your thesis with the existing body of research on your topic, show what your research adds to critical opinion of the composer in question, or point to related areas in which similar research would be appropriate. Be careful not to go overboard in your conclusion. Some students, relieved to find themselves near the end of the paper, get carried away in their conclusions and lapse into flowery or exaggerated language about the world-shaking importance of this particular topic. Provide a logical and forceful closing for the reader, then stop. As you create your outline, think about an effective conclusion for your paper.

Revising the Outline

Once you have a tentative outline, stop and take a critical look at it. In my experience, the problems pointed out by the committees that read theses and dissertations are almost always outline problems; material appears in the wrong place, the order is not logical, the emphasis is wrong, some material is not related to the project's thesis, or some necessary material is missing. It is much easier to modify the design and order of your paper at the outline stage than it is at the later stages of the draft or final copy. Check the outline carefully for unity, coherence, and logical flow. Experiment with a different order within the body of your paper. Would your thesis be more convincing if the order of supporting arguments were changed? Is the last argument the weakest or the strongest? Is there a weak argument that might better be left out? Is there anything in the outline that is not related to your thesis and therefore has no place in this paper? Is there a subject that is discussed in several different places, and would it make more sense to combine those discussions in one place? Tinker with your outline; try a different order; experiment. The more logical, coherent, and forceful your outline is, the more logical and convincing the paper will be. The time you devote to revising your outline will pay off in a stronger and more effective paper.

The computer may not be the most effective tool for the brainstorming process that is part of constructing an outline. Some writers were trained to jot down ideas in the form of spokes growing from a central thesis or main point, or in some other format that does not lend itself to a computer screen. On the other hand, most word-processing programs can help you organize ideas into headings and subheadings and produce a clear outline. Whatever system you use, the outlining phase is crucial and will have an enormous effect on the success of your paper.

WRITING THE DRAFT

After you have designed an outline that works, with everything in its proper place, sit down, face the blank screen, and start writing what you want to say. Assuming that you have built into your plan sufficient time for editing and revising, your concern at the draft stage is just to put your ideas in written form, imperfect or not, to create a preliminary version that you can work with. If you feel blocked when you try to start with the introduction, begin with the body of the paper, and return later to write the introduction. The important thing is to complete the draft.

The computer is by far the most efficient way to draft a paper, provided that you can compose at a keyboard. The better your keyboard skills are and the more fluent you are in using the features of your word-processing program, the easier it is to concentrate on what you want to say; you don't have to worry about the location of the next letter or which command to use to correct a mistake. Assuming you can type rapidly and accurately, the computer makes it possible to draft like the wind—the way the machine "wraps" the text to the next line for you, moves on to the next page, and numbers pages as you go lets you concentrate on what you want to say and draft large chunks of the paper in a relatively short time. Bear in mind that this is only a draft, not the final version you will submit. Do not allow yourself to get bogged down by typographical errors, misspellings, or awkward sentences. You can always make editorial changes and revisions at a later stage, but first you have to have a completed draft. The draft is the raw material that you will refine and polish to produce the final paper.

It makes sense to draft your paper in the correct format for college papers; that way, you can see how long your paper will be and more or less how it will look. The next chapter discusses details of correct format; here I suggest that you set up the proper margins, font, and spacing before you begin the draft rather than waiting until you are ready to print your final copy. Don't depend on your word-processing program to set up the format for you; the default formats that appear automatically on the screen probably will not be correct for college papers.

Finally, whenever you are working at a computer, whether drafting or editing, the basic rule is save, save, save. Set the program to save your work automatically every ten or fifteen minutes, and get in the habit of saving frequently yourself. A single keystroke or click on an icon takes no time and will keep your hard work from disappearing. Anyone who has ever used a computer can tell horror stories about losing large amounts of work because of a power surge, a power outage, or a computer malfunction of some sort. The rule is simple: Save—stuff happens. If you approach your professor with a tearful tale of losing hours of work, you will probably get some sympathy, because we have all suffered similar losses, but your story will not work as a valid excuse. The harsh truth of the matter is that the disaster was at least partially your own fault, since you could easily have prevented it by saving frequently.

Musical Examples

While you are writing the draft, or even earlier, in the outline stage, you should pick out the exact points in your paper where musical examples are necessary or appropriate, and how you will deal with them. In papers whose focus is analytical, it is usually helpful to include musical examples; a carefully chosen musical example may be more effective than several pages of descriptive prose. If you are trying to make a point about a striking cadence, an unusual modulation, or a particularly charming melodic idea, show the reader the music, along with your explanation.

There are several ways to include musical examples in your paper. If you have the necessary computer skills, the best way is to write out the passage in one of the music-writing programs and import it into your text at the proper place. You can also photocopy a few measures or a portion of a score that will illustrate your point and insert them into your paper in the proper place. Always consider clarity first; the examples should clearly support your point, not confuse the reader. It is difficult to extract useful musical examples from some kinds of scores; oversize Romantic orchestral scores, for instance, are not only difficult to photocopy but also difficult to read, and may be confusing or distracting to your reader. Some twentieth-century scores are also difficult to photocopy. It might be better in such situations to prepare a reduced score or some sort of diagram to illustrate your point. When you use photocopied examples, be sure they contain all the information the reader needs to make sense of them. If the measures you copy do not include clefs or key signatures, add them. Prepare photocopied musical examples before you print the final version of the paper so that you can leave sufficient space for each example. Attach photocopied examples firmly to the page with double-stick tape or by some other means. Once the examples are taped or glued in place, you may decide to photocopy the pages that contain them and insert those photocopied pages in the copy you submit. The examples in the photocopy then become a permanent part of the page, and the resulting page looks cleaner and more professional.

Sometimes the best way to illustrate the point you are making is to add analytic annotations to a photocopy of the score. Some students have a talent for graphics and can mark a score in such a way that the reader immediately sees the point the writer is trying to make. In the hands of others, marked scores come out looking like Beethoven sketches, with the musical notes and the point of the example obscured by sloppy or unclear markings. Never rely on a marked score alone to make your point about the organization of a work; there must always be some verbal explanation as well. Finally, musical examples, whether they appear in the text or in an appendix, must be clearly captioned so that the reader knows exactly what each example represents. The reader must be told the specific work, movement, and measure numbers of each example and must know precisely where the example fits into the text. We will discuss these details in the chapter on format.

Diagrams, Graphics, and Tables

You might consider designing your own diagrams or graphic representations of musical events. Diagrams can be extremely useful, particularly in questions of large-scale structure, provided that they are clear and make the point effectively. One can diagram the structure of the first movement of Bach's *Brandenburg Concerto No. 5,* for example, on a single page, whereas the *Bach-Gesellschaft* edition of the score occupies twenty-two pages. A table might be an effective way to show how the cantus firmus is used in the various movements of a Renaissance Mass, to represent the loose or unusual structures sometimes found in Romantic symphonic works, or to depict the structure of an unusual contemporary work. The point is always clarity and effectiveness. Will this diagram or graphic analysis be clear to the reader? Is this the best way to communicate the point I am trying to make? Does my diagram make sense, or does it need further modification to be clear? You can always test the clarity of a diagram by trying it out on a knowledgeable friend. If it makes the point clearly, it helps the paper enormously. If it does not, tear it up; it will only detract from the effectiveness of your paper.

Footnotes

While you are writing the draft, you must decide where footnotes are needed, insert the footnote numbers in your text, and write the notes as you write the text so that everything matches up correctly. The key is to be precise and systematic early in the process. We will deal with details of footnote format, along with other format issues, in Chapter 5. Here we will discuss when you should include footnotes and where they should be located in the finished paper.

Once you understand the purpose of footnotes, the rules about them make perfect sense. Footnotes are included in a paper to establish that the writer has some basis for the assertions he or she makes, and so that the writer can acknowledge indebtedness to the authors and ideas discovered in the process of research. The idea is that readers, if they wish, can go to the sources themselves to check the information or to pursue related lines of investigation. There are two extremes to be avoided—too few footnotes and too many footnotes. Some students include very few footnotes, even when they are obviously repeating information they discovered in their research. This omission, even if it is done carelessly or without intention to deceive, constitutes plagiarism, the use of the words of others without giving them credit; see the discussion of plagiarism later in this chapter. Other students footnote nearly every sentence, a practice that is both tiresome and unnecessary. Some general guidelines may help students to deal with this question.

First, every direct or indirect quotation must have a footnote. If you quote someone directly, copying the quotation word for word, within quotation marks, you must include a footnote that tells exactly where that quotation appears, citing the book or article, publication information, and the page where the quoted material appears in the original source. If you cite someone's opinion indirectly, without quoting that person's exact words, you still need a footnote to support your claim that the person actually said what you ascribe to him or her. The following sentence is an example of indirect quotation.

> Stuckenschmidt claims that Schoenberg first conceived the idea for *Pierrot Lunaire* in 1910, whereas Rufer cites a letter to Berg, dated October 1912, as the earliest indication that he intended to set these poems.

The writer here states as a fact that these two well-known experts made these statements. Even though the writer has not quoted their exact words, the reader still wants to know how the writer knows that these earlier authors actually said these things. You cannot write a sentence like this without adding a footnote listing the exact places in the writings of Stuckenschmidt and Rufer where they make these claims. The footnote must cite the appropriate books or articles, including information about the place and date of publication, as well as the pages on which these statements can be found. Readers should be able to check the sources themselves if they are not sure that the writer has correctly represented them or if they want to pursue the matter further.

Second, matters of common knowledge do not require footnotes. This rule can be slippery—how exactly does one determine what fits under the rubric of "common knowledge"? At the extremes, the answer is fairly obvious.

Beethoven composed nine symphonies.

J. S. Bach died in 1750, after a long and productive career.

Those sentences hardly need footnotes; anyone who has even a smattering of knowledge about classical music knows these things already. Adding a footnote to these sentences would be naïve and would mark the writer as an inexperienced researcher. On the other hand, consider this sentence:

Later in his life, Stravinsky regretted the fact that people associated him with his works in late Romantic style, such as *Firebird*.

That sentence certainly requires a footnote. The reader wants to know how you can claim to know what was going on in Stravinsky's mind and where you found this information. You have to add a footnote to this sentence, citing the source of your information. Between these two extremes, use your own common sense about the common-knowledge issue. It is helpful to keep in mind the audience for whom the paper is intended. Rather than trying to guess what your instructor might consider common knowledge, imagine yourself presenting your paper to your classmates. What is general knowledge to a group of music majors in a music history class is different from general knowledge among the population at large or a typical audience at a concert. Do not footnote what would be obvious to your colleagues. When in doubt, it is better to err on the side of including too many footnotes rather than too few.

One helpful way to avoid obtrusive numbers of footnotes is to use a general footnote for a section of a paper rather than attaching a footnote to each sentence. If your paper includes a biographical sketch of a composer that is based on one or two sources, for example, it is not necessary to include a separate footnote to support each item of information—date of birth, education, positions, important works, and date of death. You can write a single footnote referring the reader to the sources in which you found the biographical information, making clear that the note refers to all the information in that section. If an analytical section makes use of published analyses, you might list them in a single note at the beginning of the section and thereafter footnote only direct or indirect quotations. The best way to get a sense of proper footnote use is to read articles in scholarly journals; the scholars who write them and the editors who approve them understand correct footnote practice. Note as you browse through journal articles that the footnotes tend to cluster at the beginning of the article, where authors are likely to list other publications that have dealt with this topic and the primary materials on which their research is based. Footnotes appear less frequently after the first few pages, as authors move into the discussion of their own findings.

A final concern about footnotes is where they should be placed in the finished paper. The rules for theses and dissertations generally require that the footnotes be placed, as the name indicates, at the bottom of the page, rather than grouped as "endnotes" at the end of each chapter or at the end of the study. One practical reason for that requirement is that dissertations sometimes circulate in microfilm form; if the notes are at the end, it is inconvenient to scroll back and forth through hundreds of pages of text each time the reader wants to check a footnote. In other projects, endnotes may appear at the end of each chapter, or all together at the end of the text, before the bibliography. Using endnotes rather than footnotes is usually acceptable in undergraduate papers; check with your instructor to see what his or her policy is.

Word-processing programs handle footnotes with ease and place them wherever you want—at the bottom of the page, at the end of a chapter of a longer project, or at the end of the paper. You might want to put them at the bottom of the page in the draft stage so that you can check them against your text as you edit. If you wish, you can move them to the end before submitting the final copy. Word-processing programs also are very good about keeping track of footnotes as you make changes during the editing process. Whenever you add, remove, or move a section of text, the program will automatically add, remove, or move the footnotes that go with that section, making sure that the footnotes stay where they belong and changing the numbers when it is necessary. The complicated business of dealing with footnotes is one of the main reasons we should be grateful that word-processing programs were invented.

Bibliography

The last section of your draft is the bibliography. Assuming that during the research stage you kept a detailed list of all the sources you used, with the necessary publication information, preparing the bibliography is a simple matter of listing those sources in alphabetical order by author's last name and checking to be sure that the format is correct and consistent. Questions of bibliography format will be discussed, along with other format issues, in

Chapter 5. At this point, we need to discuss what should and should not be included in your bibliography.

There are different points of view on what should be included in a bibliography. The strictest position allows only those works cited in the body of the paper to be listed in the bibliography. In other words, only those publications that actually appear in the footnotes should be listed in the bibliography. A less strict position allows those publications that the writer used to be included in the bibliography, whether or not they are cited in the footnotes. The most inclusive position allows the listing of any sources the writer has run across, whether or not the writer had access to them. Check to see what your instructor's policy is about limiting the bibliography to materials you have quoted or actually seen. If one goal of the project is practice in the process of doing research and assembling a bibliography, the instructor might want you to include as many items as you can, whether or not you have consulted them.

A related issue is that of secondhand references. Let us imagine that in the course of your research you constantly run across references to one particular important source—let us call it book A. From the frequency and deference with which it is mentioned, it is clearly a central source, something you would certainly consult if you could. Let us further imagine that book A is unavailable to you but a section of it is quoted in book B, which you did find. Should you list both book B and book A in your bibliography? If you decide to list book A, are you cheating, creating the impression of direct knowledge you do not have? If you don't list book A, are you leaving yourself open to the charge of being a careless researcher, unaware of a central source? In such cases, I think it is fair to list book A. If you feel uncomfortable about listing an important publication that you have not actually seen, one solution is to list it and add an annotation such as "not available for this study." That way, the reader knows that you are aware of the existence of this important source but cannot accuse you of creating the false impression that you have actually used it.

One last important reminder. It is a mistake to pad a bibliography with questionable items just to make it look longer. Don't list the sources you used for reports in high school, such as general-purpose encyclopedias or books written for record collectors or young students. Never list your music history textbook in a bibliography; the whole point of research is to go beyond readily available sources of information. Including inappropriate items is another way to mark yourself as a naïve beginner.

Finally, the instructor may ask you to annotate your bibliography—that is, to include brief critical comments on some or all of the items. Helpful annotations point out the special advantages or the limitations of each publication. Comments like "a definitive biography, based on newly discovered primary sources," or "particularly useful for its analyses of major works," or "extensive material on the composer's political views, based on newly translated correspondence" not only show that you are a discerning researcher but also provide useful information for the reader who may want to pursue related research questions in those same sources. Annotated bibliographies are standard assignments in some graduate courses; they may be required at the undergraduate level also, and students should know what they involve.

EDITING AND REVISING THE DRAFT

After some hard work at the keyboard, you now have a file containing a complete draft of your paper on your hard drive, or on an external disk if you worked in the school computer room or on a friend's computer. The draft is an early stage of the paper, not the finished product you will hand in; it is raw material and probably needs extensive editing, revising, and polishing. The more effort you put into this process, the better your paper will be, so allow a large block of time for editing and revising. It often takes longer to polish a paper than it does to produce a draft, particularly for those who get into a creative frenzy and write drafts quickly. It is also helpful to let the draft "cool off" several times—that is, to put it aside for a while between editing sessions. When you return to a draft after a few days, it is easier to see the mistakes and awkward phrases that need revising. It is also easier to be more objective about questionable passages. The sentence that seemed not only perfectly clear but even ringing and eloquent when you drafted it at two in the morning may sound embarrassing or pretentious a few days later.

Computers and Editing

I pointed out earlier that working at a computer is the ideal way to draft a paper, provided you have good typing skills. Word-processing programs are even more powerful and helpful for revising and editing. It is strange that more students do not take advantage of the editing capability that word-processing programs provide; it is an incredible waste of expensive and sophisticated equipment to use a computer only to bang out a clumsy draft. Word-processing programs are wonderful for editing. You can move sentences or paragraphs around easily, change a word or two and then change your mind and go back instantly to the original wording, and, in general, fuss with your paper until you have it just the way you want it, all without ever retyping. If you discover that you have misspelled an important name or technical term throughout your draft, or decide that you want to replace a term with a better one, you can use the "find and replace" function to locate every appearance of the word and change them all in a second or two. Learn what your word-processing program can do, and put its power to work. If you don't have the time to master a word-processing program during the school year, take the time during a break to learn all the things it can do for you. The time you spend mastering a program will save you countless hours, raise the level and professionalism of your work, and probably improve your grades.

Finally, during the editing process, it is crucial to remember the basic rule: Save, save, save. Editing is hard work, and it is very satisfying to get a paragraph or section to say exactly what you want it to say after an hour of trying alternative wordings, moving words and phrases around, breaking up and moving sentences, and all the other work of revising. Nothing is more disheartening than watching the results of your hard work vanish because you forgot to save.

Checking Spelling and Grammar

Word-processing programs are usually equipped with tools to check spelling and grammar. These tools can be very helpful, provided that you understand what they can and cannot do and how they work. The spell-checking tool comes with a built-in dictionary against which it checks the words it sees in your prose. If a word does not appear in its dictionary, it stops, notifies you, suggests a few similar words you might have meant, and waits for you to decide. If you see that you misspelled the word, you can select one of the suggested alternatives and click "change," and the corrected word pops into your sentence. If the checker does not recognize a name or a useful technical term, you can click on "add" and the word will be added to the dictionary; the spell-checker will recognize it the next time it appears. If the word is an unusual one that you do not want to save, you can click "ignore" and go on to the next problem.

Naturally, spell-checkers cannot hold every possible word in their dictionaries. They stop, for example, on most proper names; if you think you might use a particular name again, add it to the dictionary. As you would expect, technical terms and foreign words also cause the checker to stop and question you—in fact, any unusual word will stop the checker. Mine stopped at "musics," never having encountered the plural form before; it also stopped at "Eb," meaning "E-flat," suggesting that perhaps I meant to write "Ebb." You cannot assume that the built-in dictionary is the final authority on questionable and evolving matters such as hyphenation. I wrote "upper-case," with a hyphen, in a draft; the spell-checker noticed it and suggested "upper case," two words with no hyphen; a reliable dictionary listed the preferred spelling as "uppercase," a single word with no hyphen. The responsibility for final decisions is always the writer's, and you still need a good dictionary. Still, it is well worth the time it takes to go through the process carefully, considering each reaction thoughtfully, and adding the words you will continue to use. Think of the advantages. The checker will find every typo, every case of transposed letters, single letters when doubles are correct, and vice versa, and do it quickly. New technology creates new responsibilities; now that it is easy to eliminate typos, there is no excuse whatsoever for turning in a careless draft filled with misspellings.

Grammar checkers, as you can imagine, are somewhat slower and more complicated than spell-checkers, since the problems they are designed to identify are not as straightforward as incorrect spellings. Sometimes a grammar checker does not make suggestions but merely points out things you might want to take a second look at, such as troublesome words like "there" and "their." My tendency to draft long sentences punctuated with semicolons stops the grammar checker every time. Although I was aware of this tendency, it is still helpful to see exactly how often these long sentences appear. The grammar checker also stops at all sentences in the passive voice, in case you want to change them. In addition, it looks for some things you might not expect, such as extra spaces and punctuation problems. Grammar checkers are surprisingly helpful with small details as well as the larger questions of sentence structure.

The careful writer should take advantage of these devices, aware that a spell-checker or a grammar checker cannot understand all the subtleties of language, particularly technical terms and foreign terms, and that, handy as they are, such tools cannot mend everything. The writer cannot simply delegate the responsibility for turning a problematic draft into beautiful prose. Use these tools for what they can do, and trust them on mechanical details; both tools can save you from countless embarrassing typos and mistakes.

The Editing Process

No one writes perfect drafts; therefore, editing is crucial to the success of your paper. The quality of your finished paper will depend to a great extent on the amount of work you put into this essential step.

As you begin editing your draft, you need to assume a different mental attitude from the one you assumed while creating the draft. At this point, your role is not creator but critical reader, questioning everything about your draft—the logic of its organization, every word, every phrase, every argument. You must be prepared to shuffle paragraphs or sections if moving them will make your argument more effective, to throw out sentences or whole paragraphs if they do not work, even, as a last resort, to delete the whole draft and start again. It is much better to discover and correct your own bad writing than it is to see it circled in red when the paper is returned to you.

When you are editing your draft, criticize your work from several different points of view. You will probably have to read through the draft several times, working on different issues with each pass. During the first reading, concentrate on unity and coherence, looking at the entire paper as a unit and questioning the order and effectiveness of your arguments. Have you said exactly what you wanted to say, or does your prose wander around, skirting the central issues without ever getting to the point? Are the arguments in the proper order, or does the draft ramble? Do you keep returning every few pages to matters you have already discussed? Are there discussions of some issues in several places, and should those discussions be combined in one place? Where is the most effective place for that combined discussion? Would your arguments be more effective in a different order? Are there abrupt shifts from topic to topic, or from argument to argument? Do you need to add some transitional material to make clear that you are shifting to a new subject or argument? Try to approach your work as if you were reading it for the first time. Can you follow the train of thought as it is laid out in the draft? Are there gaps in the logical argument, assumptions that are never clearly explained? Do you know at all times where you are in the argument? Is it clear where each section fits in the overall progress of the argument?

To deal with these questions, you need to view the paper as a unit, concentrating for the moment on the big picture and ignoring problems in the wording and writing style. If you plunge immediately into the detailed work of correcting typos and misspellings or rewriting awkward sentences, you may find it difficult to keep the big picture, the thesis and argument, in your mind. Checking for unity and coherence should be done early in the editing process, since it is obviously a waste of time and effort to revise and polish the wording of a paragraph that you have to delete later because it does not advance your thesis. Before you expend precious time and energy to polish a paragraph or section, you should be fairly certain that it will still be there in the final version of the paper.

On a second pass, revise your draft at the level of detail, correcting typos and asking yourself whether this word, this phrase, this sentence says what you want to say or whether you should delete it and try another way. Note the cases of weak wording, the awkward phrases, the sentences whose syntax is jumbled and unclear, and the paragraphs that may need to be completely rewritten, and then tackle each of those problems in turn. It may take several days or evenings of hard work to polish the draft; the process is not over until you feel confident that your words say exactly what you want them to say, with the clarity and emphasis you intended.

At some point, read the paper aloud to yourself. Some mistakes, particularly jumbled syntax and pretentious or flowery language, become embarrassingly obvious when you read your prose aloud. It is true that written style and spoken style are two different things. Still, if one of your sentences always comes out wrong when you try to read it aloud, or you cannot get through it without stumbling, you can assume there is something wrong with your syntax. If you, the person who wrote it, cannot read it convincingly, the reader will not be able to make sense of it either. Jumbled syntax is often an indication that the idea is not clearly formed in your mind. When you run into a tangled and confusing sentence in your draft, back up, think about exactly what you are trying to say, and then devise a way to say it clearly and effectively.

One final note about the editing process. Once you have finished editing on the screen, it is a good idea to print a copy of the paper and make one last pass through the hard copy. Some editing tasks are easier to do on hard copy than on the screen. When you want to compare a section early in your paper with a later section, for example, it is much easier to put those pages side by side than to scroll back and forth through several intervening pages. Since the individual letters and spaces in your text may look different in the hard copy from the way they do on the screen, it may be easier to notice and correct typos, spelling errors, and extra or missing spaces. If that first hard copy turns out to be perfect, you can always hand it in as your final copy.

Chapters 7 and 8 will discuss some principles of effective writing and ways to improve your wording and sentence structure during the editing process.

PRINTING

After extensive editing, your computer screen should show you exactly the way your final paper will look, revised, polished, with parts moved around and reassembled, everything just the way you want it. It then should be a simple matter of pushing the "Print" button to produce your final hard copy. The chief requirement of your printed copy is that it be clear and legible. Most printers available today produce wonderful copies. The only printing problem that I have seen lately is that some students do not replace their printer cartridges frequently enough, so that their papers vary in darkness and clarity from page to page. Either maintain your printer in optimum condition or transfer the file containing your paper to a disk, take it to the school computer room, and print your paper on the equipment provided by the school.

PROOFREADING

The writing process is still not complete when the final hard copy is in your hand. You may still need to paste in photocopied musical examples and check to see that all the examples are in their proper places and clearly captioned.

There is one remaining important step—proofreading. You cannot assume that everything is perfect in your printed copy. As I mentioned in a previous section, some problems show up more easily in hard copy than on a screen. You need to give your paper one final read, just to be sure that the pages are in the proper order and correctly numbered, the musical examples are where they belong, and there were no glitches in the printing process. When students have already spent so much time on research, writing, and editing, it is hard to understand why they skip this final stage. Proofreading does not take very long; correcting any mistakes you find may take more time. You will have to go back into your file, make the necessary corrections, and print the corrected page or section again. Depending on the nature and extent of the mistakes and how they affect the pagination, you might even have to reprint a large section or the whole paper.

Pride in your work necessitates careful attention to this final quality check. It makes no sense to save the few minutes it would take to proofread, since any errors that remain in the final copy will detract from the effectiveness of your paper, no matter how much time and effort you have put into the earlier stages. A paper prepared with care at all stages, including proofreading, will represent your best work, communicate your ideas as clearly and effectively as possible, and prove that you are a competent researcher, capable of producing professional-quality work.

KEEP YOUR FILE

Assuming you have worked carefully and diligently to produce a first-class paper, you will want to keep the file or disk containing your paper. Although professors seldom lose papers, they may take a long time to return them or not return them at all. You may very well want to have a copy of your paper in the future, for a variety of reasons. For example, you might need to submit examples of your work if you decide to apply for admission to graduate school. If your paper is returned to you covered with corrections and criticism, that probably is not the version you want to send off with your application. On the other hand, if it comes back with an A+ and a paragraph of glowing praise on the title page, you can submit that copy to the graduate school. Even if graduate school is not in your plans at the moment, it still makes sense to save the papers that represent your best work.

PLAGIARISM

Writing a research paper always involves using the ideas of others; among other things, research involves discovering what the secondary literature has to say about your topic. It would make no sense to start from scratch, ignoring all the useful information and insight already available in print. When you use the ideas of another writer, however, you must always give credit to the source of those ideas and cite in a footnote the exact place where you found the words or ideas. Presenting the words or ideas of another writer as your own work constitutes plagiarism, a serious breach of academic ethics. We need to look briefly at exactly what constitutes plagiarism and at the consequences that follow when plagiarism is detected in the academic world.

The definition of plagiarism is clear enough—using the words and ideas of another writer without giving proper credit to the source. Determining exactly what actions fall under that definition, however, confuses some students, perhaps because there are several ways to commit plagiarism. The most obvious way is to submit as your own work a paper you purchased from one of the unethical organizations that advertise on the Internet or in campus newspapers. No student on earth would argue that that sort of action is legal or ethical. Most cases of plagiarism are subtler than that, however. Commonly, a student submits a paper that is partially his or her own work but also contains paragraphs or sections copied verbatim from uncredited sources, creating the impression that the material appropriated from elsewhere is the student's own work. That is plagiarism, whether or not the student actually intended to claim that the copied words are his or her own work; the crime is in the act itself, not the student's intention. In academic papers, every quotation, either direct or indirect, must be accompanied by a footnote citing the source of the quotation. Further, it is possible to commit plagiarism even if you do not copy the exact words of another author. If you paraphrase an idea you find in another's work—that is, state it in your own words— without citing the source, you are still guilty of plagiarism. Even if the words are more or less your own, the idea was originally someone else's, and the original author must be credited for the idea.

The second thing you need to be aware of is the seriousness with which academic institutions regard plagiarism. In academia, plagiarism is a serious breach of academic ethics, regarded as seriously as, for example, stealing a final examination from a professor's office. The standard punishment for plagiarism is a failing grade for the paper and probably for the course. In addition, colleges and universities require that cases of plagiarism be reported to a committee on student conduct. Once the committee rules that the student is guilty of plagiarism, it usually questions the student's fitness to continue in the program, and sometimes recommends academic probation or even expulsion. No matter how desperate things seem, there are no circumstances that could possibly justify the risk of trying to pass off someone else's words or ideas as your own. If the fraud is detected, your college career could come to a sudden and disgraceful end. Students caught red-handed sometimes protest that they did not intend to plagiarize, that they acted inadvertently, that they did not understand the rules, or that the punishment is too harsh for what they consider a minor offense. Those arguments are of no use whatsoever; the crime is in the act, not the perpetrator's intent. Perhaps you think you can manipulate your professor if you get in a jam, or that well-timed tears will save you, but be aware that the harshest reaction will come not from your professor but from the university committee that oversees academic conduct. If you think academia takes plagiarism too seriously, remember that in the publishing world, plagiarism is an actionable crime resulting in lawsuits, huge settlements, and permanent disgrace for the guilty party. Nobody takes plagiarism lightly, and protesting innocence or ignorance is not an adequate defense.

You should also be aware that plagiarism is usually not difficult to detect. In the case of papers bought from illegal paper mills, your professors get those same ads and can find the same Internet sites you can; besides, do you really think that your professor will not notice that the paper is not written in your style? In the case of papers partially written by the student and partially plagiarized, remember that the students who are most tempted to plagiarize are those who have difficulty writing convincing prose. How hard do you think it is to notice a sudden break between the halting style of the student's prose and the polished and eloquent style of a published expert? Chains of subordinate clauses, complex and elegant parallel constructions, and abstruse technical terms used only by experts are not found very often in student prose—certainly not in the prose of students who are deficient in basic writing skills. Sometimes desperate students make silly mistakes, such as copying prose from British sources, complete with telltale British spellings ("colour" and "organise," for example), British idioms, and ways of punctuating that that are exclusively British. I once found in a student paper the German word *Durchfürung*, an old term for what we call "development." There it was, nestled in a patch of suspiciously flowery and Victorian prose. The paragraphs preceding and following this strange section were barely literate, making the plagiarized patch stand out even more. I called the student in and asked him what the German term meant; he had no idea, and immediately admitted that he plagiarized. Some of these cases would be comical if they were not so serious and did not have such tragic consequences. Forewarned is forearmed; if you have gotten yourself into such a hopeless jam that you actually contemplate desperate measures such as plagiarism, you should at least understand fully how serious the consequences can be.

CONCLUSION

The process of writing a first-class paper is long, involved, and time-consuming, a far cry from the desperate scramble a day or two before the deadline or the one or two frantic evenings that some students think is sufficient to produce a decent paper. The process of writing a paper, including the research phase, occupies several weeks at least. Even the process of writing the draft, editing, revising, printing, and proofreading, as discussed in this chapter, takes more than a few evenings' work. Remember always that no one writes perfect drafts, and turning a draft into a polished paper is a long and complex task. The quality of the paper you turn in will be in direct proportion to the amount of time and effort you put into producing it. Provided that you have done adequate research and have thought carefully about the topic, your paper will succeed or fail as a direct result of the time and care you expend in the process of drafting and revising. If you work hard at these steps, your finished product will be something you can be proud of, work that you know will meet the highest academic standards.

CHAPTER 5

Questions of Format

FORMAT FOR COLLEGE PAPERS

There are standard rules for formatting a college paper. These rules may seem archaic, but whether they make sense to you or not, you must follow standard practice if you want to be taken seriously and demonstrate your professional competence. In another part of the musician's world, recital etiquette has its own long-standing rules about dress and behavior, which may also seem archaic or pointless. Nevertheless, in both cases, if you want to be taken seriously and judged as a professional, you have to follow accepted practice.

The format for a research paper is generally the same within general areas of study such as the arts and the humanities; other fields have their own rules for format issues. In the natural and social sciences, for example, it is customary to use "author-date" citation, in which works are cited by placing the author's last name and the date of publication in parentheses within the text rather than in footnotes or endnotes. Both "humanities style," which uses footnotes or endnotes and a bibliography, and the "author-date" style are explained in detail in the Turabian guide and in *The Chicago Manual of Style* (see the Preface of this book). To complicate the situation further, the Modern Language Association has developed its own version of author-date citation, called "MLA style." This chapter discusses the humanities format, as well as some of the special problems in referring to music. Note at the outset that there are few absolute rules; there are usually several ways to handle certain details, all within the range of correct standards.

There are three basic principles to remember about format questions. First, be consistent. If you decide to follow Turabian's model for one footnote, then follow it for all footnotes. Second, be logical; the purpose of footnotes and bibliographies is to be helpful to the reader. Be sure that your notes are helpful rather than confusing, and if you cannot find a model for a particular kind of citation in one of the standard style manuals, pick the most logical and helpful way to handle the question. Third, check with your instructor to see whether you have any latitude in choosing a style guide; your instructor may insist that you follow one particular style manual. When the choice of a guide is up to you, follow the rules for humanities style in Turabian or *The Chicago Manual of Style;* Turabian is the standard in most colleges, and the *Chicago Manual* is the most authoritative guide in the world of publishing. The important thing to most instructors is that you follow one of the accepted style guides and that you are consistent and logical in the way you deal with details. The worst offenses are carelessness and inconsistency.

Paper

College papers should be typed on one side only, on plain white 8½-by-11-inch paper. Do not use the paper that is standard in Britain and Europe, which is longer and narrower than the standard paper used in the United States. The rules for theses and dissertations specify paper of a particular weight with blue lines marking the borders of the text; there is no reason to use this special paper for an undergraduate project. It should be obvious that lined sheets ripped from a notebook, with the shredded perforations still attached, are not acceptable. Save your colored paper for correspondence; lavender or buff paper is out of place for a research project and is regarded as an affectation, like brown, green, or lavender ink in a business letter.

Two other kinds of paper that were common years ago are not acceptable. Lightweight "onion skin" paper is difficult to read, because it is thin and transparent. Avoid "erasable bond," which is difficult to write comments on and annoying to read, because the letters tend to rub off on the reader's hand or sleeve; your deathless prose can vanish. Any plain white typing paper will do; paper manufactured for copy machines is fine too.

Page Format

Papers are supposed to have standard margins. Turabian (14.2) specifies a margin of at least an inch on all four sides, and notes that some institutions require larger margins, particularly on the left side. That means that absolutely nothing can extend into these margins; all illustrations, including musical examples, must fit within the side margins, and neither text nor footnotes should run over into the margin at the bottom of the page.

There are practical reasons for standard margins. First, the reader needs some space in which to write corrections and comments. A wider margin on the left is useful if the paper will be bound. In addition, standard margins provide an easy gauge of the length of a paper. A double-spaced page of 11- or 12-point type with standard margins contains between 250 and 300 words, depending on the font. It is useful for writers, instructors, editors, and publishers to know, for example, that a 5,000-word paper will be about twenty pages long. If you have to read a paper to a group, you can assume that it will take a little over two minutes to read a standard page, and gauge the proper length of your paper accordingly. Nowadays, of course, your word-processing program can provide an exact word count instantly; it is still handy to know about how many words will fit on a standard double-spaced page.

Fonts

Most word-processing programs offer a wide variety of fonts and type sizes. For papers, choose a font that looks like those found in printed books. Although the names vary somewhat from program to program, choose something with a name such as Times Roman or Times New Roman, Bookman, New Century Schoolbook, Garamond, or Palatino, or any font that looks like printing. Avoid idiosyncratic fonts that are unusually spaced, too light, too dark, or too weird, and certainly avoid fonts designed to look like script. The appropriate size depends on the font; most fonts look good and are quite readable in 10-, 11-, or 12-point size. Experiment with your favorite fonts to see which sizes work best. Fonts that are unusually small or cramped are difficult to read; fonts that are too big make your paper look like a children's book or create the impression that you are trying to make your paper look longer than it really is.

Spacing

The text of your paper should be double-spaced (Turabian 14.5). Word-processing programs have several options for line spacing, and a page of text with one-and-a-half spaces between lines generally looks quite attractive. The standard practice for both college papers and manuscripts for publishing, however, is still to double-space the text. In college papers, footnotes and bibliography entries are usually single-spaced—that is, there is a single space between the lines of each entry, and a double space between entries. The practice is different in the world of publishing; publishers usually require that everything in the manuscript, including notes and bibliography, be double-spaced. Follow the recommendations of the style guide you use.

Justification

Word-processing programs offer several options for justification: left-hand, center, right-hand, and combined right-hand and left-hand justification. Do not choose combined justification. Although it creates a uniform text block on each page and a straight right-hand margin, it also creates uneven and incorrect spacing in the individual lines of text. For that reason, it is now accepted practice to avoid right-hand justification. Set your computer for left-hand justification instead, which will create an uneven right-hand margin but keep your spacing correct.

Page Numbers

The pages of your paper should be numbered in the following way (Turabian 14.6–9). If you attach a separate title page, it is not numbered; nor is the optional extra blank sheet you might insert between title page and text. In the case of long papers, the pages of introductory material (preface, dedication, table of contents) are numbered with lowercase roman numerals—i, ii, iii, and so forth. The reason for this different numbering system is that those sections, known collectively as "front matter," are not part of the text proper and are often written last, after the main body of text is completed. In most undergraduate papers, the text begins immediately after the title page, without preliminary sections; the first page of text is thus page 1. If the title appears at the top of the first page of text, rather than on a separate title page, then that first page with the title is considered page 1 but not numbered, and the following page is number 2. Within the text, pages are numbered with arabic numerals placed at the top margin, one double-space above the top line of text, either in the upper right-hand corner or at the center of the page. Do not place numbers at the bottom of the page, where they could interfere with footnotes. Number pages consecutively through the whole paper, including appendixes, notes, and bibliography. If the paper is divided into chapters, the numbering does not begin anew with each chapter but continues consecutively through the entire paper. If during the course of working on a project you store your paper in more than one file, be sure to set up the final copy so that it is consecutively numbered.

When your paper is complete, you may want to staple the pages together with a single staple near the upper left-hand corner of the pages or insert the paper into one of the covers or folders sold for this purpose, to be sure that the pages stay together and in the proper order. Remember that the instructor will probably have a large stack of papers to read. Loose pages can easily get out of order, and paper clips slip and sometimes mix papers together; your paper can easily get jumbled together with other people's projects. Another way to be sure that each of your pages is clearly identified is to set up a header including your name, a short version of the title if you wish, and the page number. Each page of your paper is then clearly identified.

FORMAT FOR QUOTATIONS

Quoting the words of recognized experts can be a very effective way to reinforce your arguments or state a point more clearly. Quotations should be used sparingly, however, and only where they will be the most effective way to argue your point. A long string of quotations does not constitute a research paper, because there is no room for you to develop and express your own ideas. An excessive number of quotations makes the reader suspicious that the writer is using the quotations to conceal the fact that he or she has nothing original or worthwhile to say.

The proper format for quotations causes problems for many students. First of all, direct quotations must be clearly marked. Citing the exact words of another author without quotation marks and a footnote acknowledging your source is unethical; see the discussion of plagiarism in Chapter 4. Different kinds of quotations are handled in different ways.

Short Quotations

A quotation is considered short when it occupies fewer than three to ten full lines, depending on which guide you read; Turabian (5.4) defines "short" as anything less than two full sentences that occupy eight lines of text. Short quotations are integrated into the body of the text and placed in quotation marks. For example:

> Rosen finds the term "recapitulation" misleading. "If we use it to mean a simple repeat of the exposition with the secondary material put into the tonic, then the whole idea must be thrown out as unclassical: this type of recapitulation is the exception rather than the rule in the mature works of Haydn, Mozart, and Beethoven."[1]

Note that the material cited must be quoted exactly, with the author's spelling and punctuation intact. One could argue that Rosen should have used a semicolon rather than a colon after "unclassical"—that is, between two independent clauses not joined by a conjunction—but when quoting another author, the writer must quote exactly. Note the order of the punctuation marks at the end of the quotation: period, quotation marks, superscript footnote number.

Block Quotations

A long quotation—anything longer than three to ten lines or, in Turabian's view, two complete sentences occupying more than eight lines—should be set off from the body of your text. Long quotations, also called "block quotes" or "extracts," are started on a new line, single-spaced (according to most style guides), and indented (Turabian 5.4). Style guides vary in describing how far to indent long quotations; most specify four or five spaces. *The Chicago Manual* (18.32) points out that it is also acceptable to indent block quotations on both the right and the left sides. If the opening of the quotation is the beginning of a new paragraph in the original source, the first line of your block quote should be indented further than the rest, just like the opening line of any paragraph. If a new paragraph begins within the block quote, indent that first line as well, but single-space between the paragraphs. When block quotations appear on the page in this special format, there is no mistaking that the quoted material is distinct from your own text. For that reason, quotation marks are not needed at the beginning or the end of block quotes; the appearance of the page makes clear that these are not the writer's own words. Since there are no quotation marks around the whole citation, material that appears inside quotation marks within the cited material is put in double quotation marks, not the single quotation marks one would normally use for a quotation within a quotation. Although it is possible to introduce a long quotation with an incomplete sentence, such as "As Rosen says," and then start the block quote on a new line, that method seems awkward. It is better to introduce the quotation with a complete sentence.

Whenever you are contemplating including a long quotation in your paper, stop and think about its effectiveness. It is generally possible to achieve the same effect in other ways, such as paraphrasing or summarizing the content of most of the quotation, and selecting one particularly strong sentence or phrase to quote. On the other hand, the long quotation may be the best way to make your point. As is true in so many matters, moderation is the rule. If you use too many long quotations, you create the impression that you are simply stringing together apt quotations that you found, rather than communicating the results of your own research and thought.

Ellipsis and Editorial Additions

If you omit some words from a direct quotation, either a short quotation or a longer block quote, honesty and accuracy demand that you signal that omission, called an ellipsis, by the use of three spaced periods to show where material was left out (Turabian 5.18–21). If the material preceding the ellipsis ends with a period or if the following material starts a new sentence, use four spaced periods. Some word-processing programs use a special character that prints three spaced dots rather than three separate periods.

> As Rosen says, "If we use it to mean a simple repeat of the exposition . . . then the whole idea must be thrown out as unclassical."

Be very careful in your use of ellipsis. The preceding example is not a legitimate use of ellipsis, since it misrepresents what Rosen said; obviously, he did not mean to say that the recapitulation is a simple repeat of the exposition. The omitted qualifying phrase, "with the secondary material put into the tonic," is essential to the sense of the quotation. Even when ellipsis does not misrepresent what the original author wrote, it can be confusing to the reader and can raise questions about your argument. The reader naturally wonders exactly what was left out, why it was left out, and how the omitted material might change the force of the quotation.

If you feel required to add something to a quotation for the sake of clarity, you must make clear to the reader that you are doing so, by putting the editorial comment in square brackets—not parentheses (Turabian 5.35). Such insertions may be necessary to supply contextual material that is not clear in the isolated sentence cited, or to supply the antecedent of a pronoun that appears in the quoted section. Square brackets, available in all word-processing programs, are the universal sign of editorial additions. Without them, you are misquoting the cited author, creating the impression that the insertion is part of the direct quotation. If you wish to clarify what Rosen means by "it" in the preceding quotation, for example, you must enclose the added antecedent in brackets.

> **Wrong:** If we use it—the term recapitulation—to mean a simple repeat of the exposition . . .
>
> **Wrong:** If we use it (recapitulation) to mean a simple repeat of the exposition . . .
>
> **Correct:** If we use it [recapitulation] to mean a simple repeat of the exposition . . .

[*sic*]

There is a special editorial comment one can insert within quotations to let the reader know that the writer is quoting the source exactly and that the mistakes that appear in the text are the responsibility of the cited author, not the writer. The Latin word *sic* ("thus") is inserted in square brackets after an apparent error, to mean, "This is the way it appears in the source." Although some experts would set *sic* in standard type, rather than in italics, Turabian (2.25) and *The Chicago Manual of Style* (6.59) recommend italics. Since it is a complete word, not an abbreviation, *sic* is not followed by a period.

> Thomas Morley, in *A Plaine and Easie Introduction to Practicall Musicke* [*sic*], takes a somewhat different approach.

In this case, *sic* is not really necessary. Since anyone with any knowledge of Elizabethan English is aware that spelling at that time was quite erratic, the [*sic*] seems overly cautious, perhaps pedantic. There are situations, however, in which this device is useful. When you are sure, for example, that a date in a quotation is wrong, you might want to use *sic* or insert the correct date in brackets so that the reader understands that you are aware of the error.

BIBLIOGRAPHY AND FOOTNOTE FORM

The following section is a summary of the detailed guidelines for formatting bibliographies and footnotes as given in the Turabian manual and the *Chicago Manual,* and is adapted from the analogous section in Wingell and

Herzog, *Introduction to Research in Music.* Note that the various guides do not always agree on every detail of a particular kind of citation, although the general principles are clear; a guide may also list more than one way of dealing with a particular issue. In these cases, you are free to follow any format found in one of the accepted guides, unless your instructor or institution insists that you follow one particular guide for school projects. In both bibliography and footnote references, you must be clear and consistent; if you choose one option for listing volume and page number of a periodical early in your bibliography, you must follow that format all the way through. Note that this section treats format issues for bibliographies and footnotes together, going through each type of resource (books, articles, etc.) in order. Note that the main difference between bibliography and footnote format is that bibliography entries are written as a series of separate "sentences," each bit of information starting with an uppercase letter and ending with a period. Footnotes, on the other hand, are written as single "sentences," with commas rather than periods in between the various bits of information and parentheses enclosing the publication information. Note also that the footnote format listed here is for the first reference in a paper; see additional note 9 under the section headed "Books" for ways to document subsequent citations of the same items.

Books

Bibliography—basic form   Author, last name first. *Title: Subtitle.* Place: publisher, year. Bibliography entries are "out-dented"—that is, the first line of each entry is flush with the left margin, and subsequent lines are indented one tab stop.

> Smith, John. *The Music of John Cage: An Analytic Guide.* New York: W. W. Norton, 1982.

Footnote—basic form   Author, first name first, *Title: Subtitle* (Place: publisher, year), page numbers, if you wish to cite a particular passage. Footnotes are indented—that is, the reference number and first line of the entry are indented one tab stop, and subsequent lines are flush with the left margin. Footnotes, unlike bibliography entries, frequently end with page numbers referring to a particular passage relevant to the issue under discussion. To refer to a single page, type the letter "p" followed by a period, a space, and the number. For several pages, "pp. 24–29" or "pp. 24–9" is clearer than the alternative "pp. 24 ff." signifying "page 24 and the following pages." Some guides allow the omission of "p." if there is no possibility of confusion. All footnotes end with a period.

> [1]John Smith, *The Music of John Cage: An Analytic Guide* (New York: W. W. Norton, 1982), pp. 132–145. OR . . . (New York: W. W. Norton, 1982), 132–145.

Additional Notes for Both Bibliography Entries and Footnotes

1. *Multiple authors.* In a bibliography, the name of the first listed author appears last name first; the names of subsequent authors are usually listed in normal order, but may also be listed with the last name first. In footnotes, the names of all authors are listed in normal order.

Bibliography
Smith, John, Walter Brown, and William Jones. *Joachim Raff, Neglected Genius.* New York: W. W. Norton, 1939.

OR

Smith, John, Brown, Walter, and Jones, William. *Joachim Raff, Neglected Genius.* New York: W. W. Norton, 1939.

Footnote
¹John Smith, Walter Brown, and William Jones, *Joachim Raff, Neglected Genius* (New York: W. W. Norton, 1939), pp. 37–56.

2. *Multiple entries by the same author.* In a bibliography, it is not necessary to type out the author's name each time. After the first entry, type a long dash in place of the author's name—Turabian (9.27) specifies an eight-space dash, and *Chicago* (15.66) says a three-em dash—followed by a period and the title, or a comma and the name of the joint author. The entries under the single author's name should be alphabetized by the first word (excluding articles) of the title; the entries by multiple authors should come after all the entries by the single author; if there are several such entries, they too should be alphabetized by title.

Smith, John. *John Cage Remembered.* Bloomington: Indiana University Press, 1994.
————. *The Music of John Cage: An Analytic Guide.* New York: W. W. Norton, 1982.
————, Walter Brown, and William Jones. *Joachim Raff, Neglected Genius.* New York: W. W. Norton, 1939.

3. *Foreign-language titles.* In both bibliography and footnotes, titles in foreign languages must include all diacritical marks and must follow the rules of capitalization of that particular foreign language. Learn how to enter diacritical marks in your word-processing program, and copy titles and foreign names exactly. For capitalization of titles in foreign languages, learn the rules for each language, or copy the title exactly as it appears in a reliable reference work. The basic rules for the languages you are most likely to cite are as follows. In German titles, capitalize the first word of the title and all nouns; in French, Italian, and Latin titles, capitalize only the first word and proper nouns. When in doubt, find the title in a reliable reference work and type it exactly the way you find it.

4. *Subtitles*. If the book has a subtitle that you wish to include in your citation, it is customary to add a colon between title and subtitle in both bibliography and footnotes. Thus, although the title and subtitle are usually printed in different styles and sizes of type on the title page of the book, without any punctuation, they are listed in bibliography and footnote entries in normal type with the added colon.

> Rosen, Charles. *The Classical Style: Haydn, Mozart, Beethoven*. . . .

5. *Additional information*. In both bibliography and footnotes, additional information, such as the number of volumes, edition number, translator, and title of the collection from which the individual volume is taken, is placed after the title and before the publication information. If you are using a later edition of a book, list the publication information for the first edition first, and then add the publication information for the edition you used. Both Turabian (8.75–76) and *Chicago* (15.132, 15.136) specify that notations such as "second edition" and "three volumes" should use numbers and abbreviations; thus, 2nd ed., 4 vols. This guide follows that system; the alternative is to write out the numbers and words: Second edition, four volumes.

Bibliography

> Smith, John, and William Jones. *Joachim Raff, Neglected Genius*. The Great Composers Series, 2nd ed., 2 vols., trans. Edward Miller. New York: Norton, 1924; reprint, New York: Dover, 1989.

Footnote

> [1]John Smith and William Jones, *Joachim Raff, Neglected Genius*, The Great Composer Series, 2nd ed., 2 vols., trans. Edward Miller (New York: Norton, 1924; reprint, New York: Dover, 1989).

6. *Place of publication*. In both bibliography and footnotes, if the place of publication is not a well-known city, such as New York, London, Paris, or Vienna, you must add the state or province for further identification. One possible exception to this rule is the location of university presses; if the name of the state appears in the name of the press, it seems pointless to specify the state after the city as well. For example, is it necessary to say "Berkeley, CA: University of California Press"? Presumably we can trust the reader to deduce that the University of California Press is probably located in California, rather than in Idaho or Mississippi. This exception is consistent with the tendency to favor brevity and simplicity in citations. When you want to specify a state within the United States, most style guides allow you to use the postal service abbreviations for states; some still insist on the full abbreviations.

> New York: W. W. Norton, 1982.

> BUT

Upper Saddle River, NJ: Prentice Hall, 1995.

Bloomington, IN: Indiana University Press, 1987. OR Bloomington: Indiana University Press, 1987.

7. *Publisher.* In both bibliography and footnotes, some writers would shorten the publisher's name as much as possible, provided that the publisher is clearly identified. Thus, instead of "W. W. Norton & Co., Inc.," one can simply write "Norton," on the grounds that the company is well known. This approach is consistent with the trend toward simplifying citations. Others would insist on citing the publisher's name exactly as it appears on the title page. In that case, one must include the full name of the company and carefully follow details of spelling and punctuation.

W. W. Norton & Co., Inc. [with an ampersand, not "and"]
Simon & Schuster [with an ampersand, not "and"]
Harcourt Brace Jovanovich [no commas, no "and," no ampersand]

The Chicago Manual of Style (15.160), taking the middle ground, recommends citing the publisher's name as it appears on the title page, omitting the initial "The" and "Inc." or its foreign equivalents at the end, and allows either an ampersand (&) or "and" (15.163). Turabian (8.59) gives the same advice, adding a note that the abbreviated system ("Norton," "Scribner," etc.) is permissible also. As usual, whatever system you follow, follow it consistently.

8. *Date of publication.* Listing the date of publication is generally a straightforward process; in modern books, the date is listed on the reverse of the title page, somewhere in the copyright information. If you use a modern edition of an older book, list the date of the first publication as well as the date of the version you used. If no date of publication is given, even in the copyright information, you may use the abbreviation "n.d." ("no date") in place of the date in the entry, or simply list place and publisher, with a comma separating them, rather than the usual colon. Listing the dates of some types of publications, such as translations and reprints of older books, can get complicated; the *Chicago Manual* (15.170) discusses some of the complications that can arise.

9. All the foregoing information regarding footnotes applies to the first citation of a work. If a work is cited a second or third time, a shorter form is used, including just enough information to make clear which previously cited work the writer is referring to. For example, if only one work by an author has been cited previously, that work can be cited again by simply using the author's last name. This practice replaces a group of Latin abbreviations and the complicated rules for their use found in older style guides—op. cit., loc. cit., art. cit., ibid., and so on.

[1]Smith, p. 422.

If more than one work by Smith has been cited previously, the writer must specify which work he or she means; the easiest way to do this is to use a shortened form of the title. For example, when several books by John Smith have been cited previously, *John Cage Remembered* can be cited in the following way in a later footnote.

> [1]Smith, *Cage Remembered,* p. 422.

The main requirement is clarity—there should be no possible doubt about which work the writer is citing.

Dissertations

Dissertations that have been published as books are cited just like other books, listing place of publication, publisher, and date as the publication information. For dissertations that have not been published, the format is different; the title is placed in quotation marks, as if the work were an article, and the degree, granting institution, and date of conferral take the place of the publication information.

Published Dissertation—Bibliography
Jones, Jane. *The Ballate of Francesco Landini.* Ann Arbor, MI: University Microfilms, 1990.

Published Dissertation—Footnote
[1]Jane Jones, *The Ballate of Francesco Landini* (Ann Arbor, MI: University Microfilms, 1990).

Unpublished Dissertation—Bibliography
Smith, Joan. "Hindemith's Early Songs." Ph.D. dissertation, University of Chicago, 1989.

Unpublished Dissertation—Footnote
[1]Joan Smith, "Hindemith's Early Songs" (Ph.D. dissertation, University of Chicago, 1989).

Articles in Dictionaries and Encyclopedias

Bibliography—basic form for unsigned articles   Editor of lexicon, last name first. *Title.* Place: publisher, date. S.v. "Title of article." "S.v." is an abbreviation for the Latin words "sub verbo," or "sub voce," meaning "under the word"; the plural form is "s.vv." This abbreviation directs the reader to the specific entry or entries the writer wishes to cite.

Slonimsky, Nicolas, ed. *Baker's Biographical Dictionary of Musicians.* 8th ed. New York: Schirmer Books, 1992. S.v. "Mahler, Gustav."

Footnote—basic form for unsigned articles   Editor of lexicon, *Title* (Place: publisher, date); s.v. "Title of article."

> ¹Nicolas Slonimsky, ed., *Baker's Biographical Dictionary of Musicians,* 8th ed. (New York: Schirmer Books, 1992); s.v. "Mahler, Gustav."

Notes

1. Sometimes a reference work has existed for a long time and several editors have worked on it. In those cases, the work may be alphabetized under its long-standing name, with the present editor listed afterward. *Baker's* is frequently listed in this way.

Bibliography
> *Baker's Biographical Dictionary of Musicians,* ed. Nicolas Slonimsky. 8th ed. New York: Schirmer Books, 1992. s.v. "Mahler, Gustav."

Footnote
> ¹*Baker's Biographical Dictionary of Musicians,* ed. Nicolas Slonimsky, 8th ed. (New York: Schirmer Books, 1992); s.v. "Mahler, Gustav."

2. In the case of larger encyclopedias such as *The New Grove Dictionary of Music and Musicians* or *Die Musik in Geschichte und Gegenwart,* which contain long articles by recognized authorities, an alternative format is to list the article by the author and title of the article. In compiling a bibliography, one often finds that books and articles by the same author who wrote the article in a lexicon are already listed in the bibliography. It makes sense to include the lexicon article in the same place under the author's name. In addition, since some of the articles in *New Grove* are book-length monographs, the authors deserve specific mention in the citation.

Bibliography—basic form for signed articles   Author's name, last name first. "Title of article." *Title of lexicon,* edition. Editor's name. Volume number, page. Place: publisher, date.

> Planchart, Alejandro. "Dufay." *The New Grove Dictionary of Music and Musicians,* 2nd ed. Edited by Stanley Sadie and John Tyrell. Vol. 7, pp. 647–664. London: Macmillan, 2000.

Footnote—basic form for signed articles   Author's name, "Title of article," *Title of lexicon,* edition, editor's name, volume number, page (Place: publisher, date).

> ¹Alejandro Planchart, "Dufay," *The New Grove Dictionary of Music and Musicians,* 2nd ed., edited by Stanley Sadie and John Tyrell, vol. 7, pp. 647–664 (London: Macmillan, 2000).

Notes on Articles in Lexicons

1. The standard guides have little to say about citing lexicons such as *The New Grove* or *Die Musik in Geschichte und Gegenwart;* their rules are clearly designed for citing well-known works such as *Encyclopaedia Britannica*. They recommend omitting the publication information when citing standard sources; the citation then lists only title, edition, and specific entry. Perhaps this system should be used for the specialized lexicons that we cite frequently in music research.

2. There are different ways to cite volume and page numbers when listing an article in a lexicon. The listing of volume and page may appear at the end of the entry, after the publication information; one can also omit the abbreviations for "volume" and "page," listing only the number of the volume, followed by a colon and the page numbers.

Bibliography

. . . . Edited by Stanley Sadie and John Tyrell. 7:647–664. London: Macmillan, 2000.

OR . . . . Edited by Stanley Sadie and John Tyrell. London: Macmillan, 2000. 7:647–664.

Footnote

[1] . . . , edited by Stanley Sadie and John Tyrell, 7:647–664 (London: Macmillan, 2000).

OR [1] . . . , edited by Stanley Sadie and John Tyrell (London: Macmillan, 2000), 7:647–664.

Articles in Periodicals

Bibliography—basic form Author, last name first. "Title of Article: Subtitle." *Title of Journal* volume number (year): page numbers.

Wallace, Robert. "Poetic and Musical Structures in the Songs of the Troubadours." *Journal of the American Musicological Society* 34 (1974): 14–32.

Footnote—basic form Author, first name first, "Title of Article: Subtitle," *Title of Journal* volume number (year): page numbers.

Citing the Entire Article

[1] Robert Wallace, "Poetic and Musical Structures in the Songs of the Troubadours," *Journal of the American Musicological Society* 34 (1974): 14–32.

Citing a Particular Passage

[1] Robert Wallace, "Poetic and Musical Structures in the Songs of the Troubadours," *Journal of the American Musicological Society* 34 (1974): 14–32; see pp. 30–32.

Note: In both bibliography and footnotes, there are several ways to list the volume and page numbers of a periodical. One option is to use roman numerals for the volume number; the disadvantage of that option is that roman numerals for numbers over twenty or thirty get very cumbersome. Whatever system you use, use it consistently. Remember also that in the case of scholarly periodicals, there is no need to list any of the other information that might appear on the title page, such as issue number or season of the year, since all the issues for a particular year are paginated continuously and eventually bound as a single volume. The only information one needs to locate the article is volume number, year, and pages.

Articles in Collections of Essays

Basic form, both bibliography and footnote   The name of the author and the publication information are dealt with exactly as they are for books. The title of the article is enclosed in quotation marks. The additional information, including the title of the collection, usually in italics, the editor's name, and the page numbers of the cited article, along with any other additional information, is listed after the title of the article and before the publication information.

Bibliography
Wilson, George W. "Monteverdi's Venetian Operas." In *The Monteverdi Companion,* ed. Denis Arnold, 332–359. Chicago: University of Chicago Press, 1987.

Footnote, Citing a Specific Page
    [1]George W. Wilson, "Monteverdi's Venetian Operas," in *The Monteverdi Companion,* ed. Denis Arnold (Chicago: Chicago University Press, 1987), 332–359; see p. 356.

Scores

In bibliographies, scores and recordings are often listed separately from the listings of books and articles. Scores are cited in both bibliographies and footnotes in much the same way as books; in bibliographies they are alphabetized by the composer's last name. In both bibliographies and footnotes, the composer's name is first, followed by the title of the work. If the work cited is part of a larger work, that title comes next, followed by the name of the editor (if there is one listed) and the usual publication information—place, publisher, and date. Footnote references make the same format changes as in the case of books.

Bibliography
Mahler, Gustav. *Das Lied von der Erde.* Kassel: Bärenreiter, 1976.

Footnote
    [1]Gustav Mahler, *Das Lied von der Erde* (Kassel: Bärenreiter, 1976).

Note: Citing scores is not always as straightforward as these examples would indicate. Scores often list editors, they may be contained in large collected sets that have their own editors, works may have nicknames (*Eroica, Farewell*) that should be listed, and so forth. Generally, just as in the case of books, any additional information is placed after the title and before the publication information. Further issues about citing musical works will be discussed later in this chapter.

Bibliography
Bach, J. S. Cantata no. 78, *Jesu der du meine Seele,* ed. Alfred Dürr. Series I, Band 2, of *Neue Ausgabe sämtlicher Werke,* ed. Johann Sebastian Bach Institut of Göttingen and the Bach-Archiv of Leipzig. Kassel: Bärenreiter, 1954–.

Footnote
    [1]J. S. Bach, Cantata no. 78, *Jesu der du meine Seele,* ed. Alfred Dürr, Series I, Band 2, of *Neue Ausgabe sämtlicher Werke,* ed. Johann Sebastian Bach Institut of Göttingen and the Bach-Archiv of Leipzig (Kassel: Bärenreiter, 1954–).

Sound Recordings

Basic form—bibliography   Composer, last name first. Title of the work or title of the recording if it is different from the title of the work, in italics. Format—analog disc, analog tape, digital disc, or digital tape. Manufacturer, number, date. If you wish to list principal performers, place that information after the title of the work and before the information about format and manufacturer.

Mahler, Gustav. *Das Lied von der Erde.* Kathleen Ferrier, mezzo-soprano; Vienna Philharmonic Orchestra, cond. Bruno Walter. Digital disc. Deutsche Grammophon, 410 715-2, 1982.

Basic form—footnote   The same kinds of format changes are made as in the case of books—the composer's name is listed first name first, commas appear between items of information, publication information (here, manufacturer and number) is enclosed in parentheses, and there is a period at the end.

    [1]Gustav Mahler, *Das Lied von der Erde,* Kathleen Ferrier, mezzo-soprano, Vienna Philharmonic Orchestra, cond. Bruno Walter; digital disc (Deutsche Grammophon, 410 715-2, 1982).

Citing Interviews, Correspondence, and E-Mail

The standard resources are not of much use for some types of specialized research, such as the study of very recent music or events. Research in these areas usually involves unusual methods, such as listening to taped interviews collected in archives or contacting knowledgeable people directly through interviews, correspondence, or e-mail. There are standard ways to cite various kinds of interviews; both the *Chicago Manual* and the Wingell/Herzog *Introduction to Research in Music* discuss these special format issues. Most undergraduate writing projects are not likely to involve this kind of research; should you find yourself involved in such a project, consult those sources to see how to cite interviews.

Interviews with experts are appropriate only when you are doing highly specialized research and only after you have exhausted all the normal channels for gathering information. Any researcher can probably find books and articles in which these experts explain their ideas. Do not impose on someone's time by firing off an e-mail inquiry, a practice now becoming popular.

Citing Electronic Resources

Chapter 3 spoke about electronic resources for research. Since the researcher can now consult on-line journals, databases, bibliographic resources, and other sources of information, we need a standard way to cite Web sites and other electronic resources. The standard style guides are experiencing some difficulty keeping up because of the rapid pace of change in this field. The fourteenth edition of *The Chicago Manual of Style,* for instance, the most authoritative style guide, has little to say on this issue. The University of Chicago Press maintains a Web site called "Chicago Manual of Style FAQ"; the acronym, as many of you know, stands for "Frequently Asked Questions." The editors note on that site that the world of electronic research has progressed too rapidly for their publication schedule. The fifteenth edition of the *Chicago Manual* is scheduled to be published in 2002 or 2003, and the editors promise to treat the citation of electronic resources in much more detail than in the current edition, which was published in 1993.

In the meantime, the editors of *Chicago* recommend the following ways of referring to electronic resources; any changes in these recommendations between now and the publication of the next edition will be noted in the FAQ Web site; the URL is <http://www.press.uchicago.edu/Misc/Chicago/cmosfaq.html>. One can also enter the search term "Chicago Manual of Style" in a browser to find the Web sites related to this publication. Following are some of the editors' recommendations—always with their qualification, "for now."

1. To avoid confusion, URLs ("Uniform Resource Locators") should be enclosed in angle brackets, as in the previous paragraph, to distinguish

them from text and to be absolutely clear about where they begin and end.

2. "On-line," when used as an adjective, always has a hyphen—thus, "an on-line journal." When "on line" is used as a prepositional phrase, it does not take the hyphen—thus, "I need to search on line to see if some other library has that score."

3. "Web" and "Internet" are treated as proper nouns and therefore capitalized. The phrase "Web site," when used as a noun, is written as two words; when used as an adjective, it is written with a hyphen.

Guides for citing electronic resources   On that same Web site, the editors of the *Chicago Manual* list guides the researcher can use for citing electronic resources. There are several Web sites in which organizations such as the Modern Language Association, the American Psychological Association, and the World Association of Medical Editors list their rules for citing electronic resources. The problem is that some of those organizations have their own special formats for all bibliographic citations; if their standard ways of citing print resources are different from those used by researchers working in the arts and humanities, there may be differences in the way they cite electronic resources as well. There are also on-line guides published by the International Federation of Libraries and Institutions and the International Organization for Standardization. The URLs for all these Web sites may be found in the Chicago Manual FAQ site cited above.

The site also mentions two books that deal with citing electronic resources; from the frequency with which these books are cited whenever these issues are discussed, one may assume that they represent current standard practice. I recommend that researchers follow one of these guides for now. When the fifteenth edition of the *Chicago Manual* appears, its guidelines will no doubt become the accepted standard, and those same guidelines will probably be duplicated in a subsequent edition of the Turabian guide. For now, the following books are the standard guides.

Li, Xia, and Nancy B. Crane. *Electronic Styles: A Handbook for Citing Electronic Information.* Medford, NJ: Information Today, 1996.
Harnack, Andres, and Eugene Klippinger. *Online / A Reference Guide to Using Internet Sources.* New York: St. Martin's Press, 1997.

General principles   Even in this interim period, while the standard guides are deciding exactly how to deal with this exploding field, there are some established principles, based on analogy with print resources and common sense, that the writer can follow.

1. Articles published in on-line journals should be cited just like articles published in print. The citation should include the name of the author, the title of the article, the title of the journal, and the volume and

number of the issue. Instead of page numbers, add the URL in angle brackets.

Bibliography

Schulenberg, David. "Some Problems of Text, Attribution, and Performance in Early Italian Baroque Keyboard Music." *Journal of Seventeenth-Century Music* 4 (1998) <http://www.sscm.harvard.edu/jcsm/v4no1/Schulenberg.html>.

Footnote

[1]David Schulenberg, "Some Problems of Text, Attribution, and Performance in Early Italian Baroque Keyboard Music," *Journal of Seventeenth-Century Music,* 4 (1998) <http://www.sscm.harvard.edu/jcsm/v4no1/Schulenberg.html>.

2. In citing other kinds of Web sites, list whatever bibliographical information is available. The order is as follows: first the name of the site's author, if it is given, and the title of the site; then the date of publication, if it is given; some guides recommend listing the date you consulted the site, since sites come and go and URLs change; the last item is the URL, exactly as it appears on the screen, enclosed in angle brackets.

Notes on Citing Electronic Resources

1. I already mentioned enclosing URLs in angle brackets to separate them clearly from the rest of the text. The *Chicago* editors also recommend that if a URL runs over to a second line, you type a space between the end of the first line and the start of the second, and do not allow the period between two items to appear at the end of a line; put it instead at the start of the second line, so that there is no confusion about exactly where the URL starts and ends.

2. The URL for the Schulenberg article cited above makes sense at a glance. It is clear that the string of characters starting with "sscm" indicates that this is the site for the Society for Seventeenth-Century Music; the home server is at Harvard, which is connected to the educational network; the subheadings continue with abbreviations for the journal and Vol. 4, No. 1. Unfortunately, not all URLs are that logical or that short; they can be difficult to remember or decipher. If you are working at your own computer, it is of course a simple matter to bookmark sites that you will want to revisit, and there is no need to commit dozens of long URLs to memory. If, however, you are working in your school's computer center, you need to carry around a list of the URLs you want to consult. You can also use a browser to locate useful URLs; the problem with that strategy is that it might take a while for you to hit on the exact search term that will lead you to the desired information.

In dealing with citations of electronic resources, just as in the case of print resources, special situations arise that call for the writer to use his or her common sense and judgment. The goals are still clarity and consistency in citing resources; cite material in such a way that interested readers can find their own way to those materials. By 2003, when the new *Chicago Manual* is available, we should have a clear standard for citations of electronic material; in the meantime, the two books listed above and these few principles should help to answer any questions that arise.

FORMAT ISSUES RELATED TO WRITING ABOUT MUSIC

The latest editions of both the *Chicago Manual* and the Turabian guide include brief sections on format issues related to music; see *Chicago Manual* 7.149–153 and Turabian 9.123–124. The standard style guides, however, do not always provide useful answers for all the technical issues that come up as we write about music, and the editors point out that many of their recommendations are not hard-and-fast rules. There are some standard practices in scholarly writing about music that run counter to the suggestions of the standard style guides. Each specific musical topic, of course, involves its own peculiar editorial questions; here I will mention some general issues that affect most writing about music.

Stylistic Periods

It is standard editorial practice in writing about music to capitalize the terms we use for the historical periods—thus, the Baroque era, the Classical period, the Romantic period. We do this to distinguish these terms from the same words used in their general senses, in usages such as "those baroque decorations," "classical music" (as opposed to popular music), or "the lyrical romanticism of a Mozart aria." This practice runs counter to the *Chicago Manual* (7.63–67), which recommends the use of lowercase initials for all such terms, unless they represent specific historical periods, such as the Renaissance or the Age of Enlightenment, or are based on proper names, such as the Victorian era. To music historians, "Baroque," "Classical," and "Romantic" do represent specific historical eras—hence the uppercase initials. Terms such as neoclassicism, impressionism, and expressionism, since they represent styles rather than specific periods of history, are not capitalized.

Referring to Musical Works

Musical works with specific titles, such as *Fanfare for the Common Man, Orfeo,* or *Die schöne Müllerin,* are easy to cite; like book titles, they are put in italics, and the writer must follow the capitalization rules of the language of the title. Things get more problematic in the case of generic titles, particularly when they also have subtitles, opus numbers, and catalog numbers, and there are several options for the ordering of all those elements. Following are some of the questions that arise when referring to musical works.

Italics or quotation marks In general, italics are used for titles of works; individual numbers or movements of larger works are put in quotation marks. Although the distinction between works of different size is clear in the following examples, the *Chicago Manual* (7.139) points out that these distinctions are arbitrary; when your discussion compares several musical works, it might be better to put all the titles in italics.

"I Know That My Redeemer Liveth" from *Messiah*

"Come scoglio" from *Così fan tutte*

Note: The second example contradicts the general rule that foreign words should be italicized unless they have become normal English words. When unfamiliar foreign words appear within quotation marks in titles, they are already clearly separated from the writer's text, and hence need not be italicized.

Generic titles Generic titles are *not* set in italic type; the generic terms are, however, capitalized when they are part of a title and left as lowercase words when they are not part of a specific title. Thus:

The Fourth String Quartet is the last quartet that Bartók wrote.

Sometimes there are several ways to list a title; the proper procedure is to cite the title exactly the way it appears in a reliable scholarly edition, or in the worklists of lexicons such as *The New Grove Dictionary*. For example, here are several ways to name the same well-known work.

Piano Concerto in C Minor, K. 491

Concerto no. 20 for Pianoforte and Orchestra in C Minor, K. 491

Concerto in C Minor for Piano and Orchestra, K. 491

One can imagine other ways of listing this same information; imagine the range of possibilities when one wants to cite a Vivaldi concerto grosso, with its list of instruments and the different numbering systems found in the three Vivaldi catalogs. In such instances, follow the two usual rules—use a reliable reference work as your authority, and be consistent.

Subtitles Many works with generic titles have customary subtitles that appear in editions of the work; such subtitles, whether they originated with the composer, critics, historians, or the public, have become an accepted part of the title. They are put within parentheses, with either quotation marks or italics, at the end of the work's title. According to the *Chicago Manual,* such subtitles are put in italics if the work is long and quotation marks if the work is short. Alternatively, all such nicknames may be put in normal type within quotation marks.

Haydn, Symphony no. 102 in E-flat Major ("Drum Roll") OR . . . (*Drum Roll*)

Schubert, Quintet in A Major for Piano and Strings ("The Trout")

Companies that produce and market recordings of classical music sometimes add subtitles to remind potential buyers that these works have crossed over into pop culture as a result of having been used as background music in films. Thus, in record stores, one can see titles such as Mozart's "Elvira Madigan" Piano Concerto, or *Also sprach Zarathustra* (The "2001" Tone Poem) by Richard Strauss. Obviously, these commercial nicknames have no place in a research paper.

Opus numbers   If numbers are included in the citation of a musical composition, the terms "op." (for "opus") and "no." (for "number") are usually not capitalized; according to Turabian and *Chicago*, they may also be capitalized, provided the writer is consistent in this matter. When a number is used restrictively—that is, to specify a particular work—it is not set off by commas; a number that follows another restrictive element in the title is set off by commas, since it then is not restrictive and merely provides additional information. If numbers are spelled out in a title, they are capitalized.

Hungarian Rhapsody no. 12, BUT Brahms's Twelfth Hungarian Rhapsody

The Sonata in E Major, op. 45, was composed in 1822; BUT The Sonata op. 45 was composed . . .

Sonata op. 31, no. 3, was composed . . .

Sonata op. 31, K. 415, was composed . . .

Naming Notes and Keys

In normal prose, musical notes or keys should be capitalized; this practice is necessary to distinguish notes from ordinary words, so that we avoid ambiguous sentences like "Chopin composed his Prelude in a flat." Note that this practice is different from the shorthand system used in analysis projects, in which uppercase "C" stands for "C major" and lowercase "c" means "C minor." In prose, always use the capital letter, and add the words "major" or "minor" if necessary. When the words "major" and "minor" appear in titles of musical works, they are capitalized.

Sonata in C Minor, BUT The development section begins in the key of C minor.

Prelude and Fugue in E OR Prelude and Fugue in E Major

Toccata and Fugue in D Minor, NOT Toccata and Fugue in d

If it is necessary in your paper to use a system of uppercase letters, lowercase letters, and superscript numbers or strokes to designate notes in different octaves, you should explain the system you are using in a footnote or the preface, and follow it consistently.

The chromatic inflections of notes ("sharp" and "flat") and the term "natural" should be spelled out as words, both in your text and in bibliographies and footnotes. Do not use the sharp sign (#) for "sharp" or a lowercase B for "flat," as in C# or Eb; after the uppercase letter naming the note, add a hyphen and then "flat," "sharp," or "natural," spelled out as words. These three words are *not* capitalized in titles; the combination of letter, hyphen, and qualifier is treated as a single term.

> Rachmaninoff's Prelude in C-sharp Minor, NOT Prelude in C# Minor, Prelude in c#, or Prelude in C Sharp Minor.

> The whole-note G-sharp in the countertenor, altered to form the double leading-tone cadence, clashes with the shorter G-natural in the upper voice.

> According to some scholars, Bach associated keys like A-flat and C minor with resignation and contemplation. NOT . . . keys like Ab and c.

Foreign Terms

As a general rule, familiar words borrowed from foreign languages should be set in roman type, and unfamiliar foreign words should be set in italics. The problem, of course, is determining which words are familiar. Style guides used to base the distinction on the dictionary; if a foreign word appears in a reliable English dictionary, it should be treated as a normal English word. Now the guides question this principle. The *Chicago Manual* (6.69) points out that no dictionary can take into account the special vocabularies of all disciplines; everyday terms in one field may be completely unfamiliar in another. In music history, terms such as "sarabande" and "sonata-rondo" are everyday words, but most people in other fields would not recognize them. In art history, "chiaroscuro" and "gouache" are common terms, although few music students are familiar with them.

Even in the field of music, besides the foreign words that everyone understands—sonata, concerto, allegro, crescendo, staccato—there is another layer of terminology that is more specialized—cantus firmus, concerto grosso, sonata da chiesa, oboe d'amore, violino piccolo. Current practice recommends italicizing these less familiar terms on their first appearance, particularly if you include a definition, and setting them in roman type thereafter.

> In the cantata *Wachet auf, ruft uns die Stimme,* Bach calls for a *violino piccolo,* a slightly smaller violin tuned a minor third higher . . . . In the duet "Wann kommst du, mein Heil?" the violino piccolo plays the obbligato line.

Another problem with these terms is forming the proper plural. The everyday terms such as "concerto" and "sonata" pose no problem, but rarer compound terms can. I think it is acceptable to write "three violas da gamba" and "two oboes d'amore," but the only plural forms I can imagine for "concerto grosso" or "violino piccolo" are the foreign forms—"concerti grossi" and "violini piccoli." If you are not sure how to form foreign plurals, of if these foreign plural forms strike you as stiff or pedantic, rewrite the sentence so that you can use the singular form of the term.

Musical Examples

There is a standard format for the title or caption of a musical example Students sometimes assume that it is redundant to provide any information with an example, since they have already introduced it in the text; that assumption is wrong for several reasons. First of all, examples cannot always be placed exactly at the spot where they are mentioned in the text; therefore, they need to be identified clearly. Even if they were located near the relevant discussion in the text, musical examples are a form of quotation and therefore must be accompanied by the same kinds of information that accompany any quotation. Each musical example should be clearly identified—there should be no doubt in the reader's mind about precisely what page of what piece he or she is looking at. Every example should therefore have a title, which includes an example number and the identification of the work quoted, including the composer's name, the title of the work, the movement, if appropriate, and the measure numbers. When you list measure numbers, remember that the abbreviation for measure is "m.," followed by a space and the appropriate number. The plural form is "mm.," again followed by a space and the numbers. Do not use "ms." to mean "measures"; "ms." is the standard abbreviation for "manuscript." Finally, the title of each example should end with a footnote number, directing the reader to a footnote that cites the publication from which the example was taken and lists the publication information for the score.

CONCLUSION

Although this chapter has devoted considerable space to questions of format, we have barely scratched the surface; look through *The Chicago Manual of Style* for a more thorough treatment. The central point to bear in mind is that there is a proper way to format and present a paper, and you can find answers to all your format questions in the standard guides. If you are careless about the format for footnotes and bibliography entries or skip the notes or the bibliography altogether, you cannot expect your paper to be treated as a serious piece of work. There is an accepted format for research papers, and your work will not be taken seriously—or may not be read at all—unless you submit it in acceptable style. Knowledge of the proper format for research papers is one of the tools of your present "trade" and one of the ways in which you demonstrate your professional competence and ability to meet the exacting standards of the world in which you have chosen to compete.

CHAPTER 6

Other Kinds of Writing Projects

Research papers are not the only written assignments you will encounter as you pursue a degree in music. Other kinds of projects involve the same challenges and skills, the same attention to research and organization of material, and the same careful preparation as writing a research paper. In addition, each of these tasks has its own special requirements; each, therefore, deserves brief discussion.

THE SEMINAR PRESENTATION

Presenting a report in a seminar is in some ways the most difficult of academic assignments. Like most people, students often feel intimidated by the prospect of addressing a group, and your peers are the most frightening group of all. Some people are blessed with a knack for speaking in a natural, lively, and persuasive way. Most of us, however, feel shy and nervous when addressing a group; unfortunately, nervousness expresses itself in various ways, none of them helpful. Some people giggle, some try to be cute or humorous, some bluster, some hide behind a stiff and formal exterior. The most effective strategy is to be prepared, be enthusiastic, and be yourself. Once you survive the experience of giving your first public lecture, it becomes much easier to organize a good presentation and present it effectively.

Since this guide is about writing, not public speaking, it is not my place here to train persuasive speakers. Granting that spoken style is different from written style, and that preparing for an oral presentation is different in some ways from the process of writing a convincing paper, there are still important similarities, and there are some useful principles to keep in mind. We will discuss each step of the process.

Research

The process of locating material for a seminar presentation is exactly the same as the research process for a paper. The fact that an oral presentation has to work within strict time limits does not mean that you can spend less time at research than you would for a paper. In fact, you might want to be especially thorough in doing research for a seminar presentation, since some time is usually scheduled for questions and discussion. You certainly want to have a command of the topic that is deep and wide-ranging so that you can answer any questions your classmates might raise. As you can imagine, nothing is more embarrassing than to find yourself fumbling around, unable to answer a question on the topic that you are supposed to be in charge of, and a weak performance in the discussion phase can negate the effect of your presentation, no matter how impressive the rest of it was. No research ever goes to waste, even if some material you discover does not fit into the presentation itself. Review the discussion of the research process in Chapter 3, and start with the basic resources listed there—library catalogs, electronic databases, dictionaries and encyclopedias, histories, biographies, and thematic catalogs. For a seminar presentation, you will also want to locate good recordings of the music in question, since you probably will want to include audio examples.

Organizing the Presentation

Once you have completed your research, the process of turning a mass of information into a logical, coherent presentation is similar to the early stages of writing a paper. The first thing you need is a logical and detailed outline; review the section on outlining in Chapter 4. A clear outline is perhaps more critical for a seminar presentation than it is for a paper. Usually, the word limit for a paper is somewhat flexible, so if you decide, even as late as the editing stage, that additional material is necessary, you can always add a page or two or a new section. In a seminar presentation, on the other hand, you have to stay within rigid time limits; if you devote a few minutes to an interesting digression, you have less time to explain your main point. You must construct a clear outline, and you must be ruthless in deleting any ideas, no matter how interesting, that do not advance your main point. As you construct and revise your outline, there are several issues peculiar to oral presentations that you should keep in mind.

Time limits   Working carefully within the time constraints is the key to planning an effective seminar presentation. Let us assume that the professor has allotted a definite time period, perhaps a half hour or an hour, to each presentation. You will probably have to stop when your allotted time is up, whether or not you have covered the material you planned to discuss. In my experience, some students do not take the time limits seriously and consequently make unrealistic plans to cover much more than it is possible to discuss in the allotted time. What happens, of course, is that the presentation is cut short and is not successful. The first time you prepare for an oral presentation, it may be difficult to estimate how much time each point will take and to put together a realistic plan for the allotted time. If you are not sure about your timing, ask some fellow students whose judgment you trust to act as the audience for a dress rehearsal. Not only will you get a better sense of pace and timing; they can also tell you whether your presentation is clear, logically organized, and easy to follow, and whether some sections need more work.

Recorded examples   Assuming that your presentation deals with some aspect of musical style, you will want to use recorded musical examples as illustrations. Because of the time limits, you need to be very selective about recorded examples; choose brief excerpts that clearly support what you are saying. A seminar presentation is not the appropriate time for an extensive survey of a composer's greatest hits. I remember distinctly one presentation in a graduate seminar years ago; the student, unable to choose between excerpts, told us at the beginning of the presentation that he had forty-five minutes of recorded excerpts that he wanted to play during his one-hour presentation. Of course, he was not able to finish his presentation. After dealing with a fraction of his planned outline, he trailed off lamely with a summary of what he would have covered had there been enough time. He sulked for the rest of the semester, angry with me for enforcing the time limits, even though all his colleagues managed to fit their presentations into the time allotted.

Recorded excerpts must be chosen very carefully and timed exactly. Although compact discs allow you to find the exact minutes and seconds you want for your starting and stopping points, it still may be more convenient to re-record your excerpts on a new compact disc or tape. Everything must be carefully planned if you want to take full advantage of your limited time; don't try the patience of your colleagues by fumbling for the excerpt you want. The time and effort you devote to preparing your musical examples will ensure that your presentation moves along briskly and creates a professional and convincing impression.

Writing every word versus speaking from an outline   As you edit and fine-tune your outline, you will need to decide whether you plan to speak from a detailed outline or write out every word and then read your text. If the instructor insists on your reading a fully written-out text, then of course you need not make this decision. If the choice is up to you, consider the advantages and disadvantages of both strategies. Writing out the full text has the obvious advantage of ensuring that you will not have to fumble for the next word or idea. The disadvantage is that reading a paper is not the same thing as speaking to a group, and listening to someone read a paper can be deadly. Although some people can turn reading a paper into a lively experience for the hearer, I generally encourage students to work from a detailed outline. The advantage is that your words seem more direct and spontaneous. Since no one but you will ever see either your outline or your text, you can devote more time to refining your outline and preparing your recorded examples and spend a little less time editing a written text. The outline should be very detailed so that you know exactly where you are going and how you plan to get there. In particular, you must know in advance exactly how you will begin and how you want to end. In fact, it may be advisable to write out your introduction and conclusion so that you get under way smoothly and wrap up the presentation with a strong conclusion rather than trailing off weakly with something like, "Well—that's about all I have to say." In your notes, you must also write out all direct quotations or give detailed directions for finding them, including book titles and page numbers. The same is true for examples or illustrations. It is deadly to sit through a long pause while the presenter fumbles through a book to find a passage he or she wants to read or show to the group.

Preparing a handout   As you work with your outline, deciding exactly what you want to cover and how you plan to proceed, you should consider assembling a handout of three or four pages to distribute to the class. There are several advantages to handouts. First, some kinds of information are much easier to understand and process by reading than by hearing. Bibliographic notes, a list of the composer's works, or an outline of the main events of a person's life are much easier for your audience to read from a page than to pick up by ear. Besides, it is useful for the listeners to have a selected bibliography for their files, should they wish to review the presentation or return to the topic at some time in the future.

You might also consider including in your handout a carefully chosen musical example or two. If all members of the class have the same measures of music in front of them, you can discuss specific details of musical style that would be difficult to make clear by your words alone; it is also much more efficient than taking the time to write examples on the board. As you put the handout together, you can mark the pages of music to draw attention to the details you plan to discuss.

Some students go to extremes in preparing handouts for seminars, as if the grade for the presentation were determined solely by the size, weight, and cost of the handout. I have seen handouts of twenty or thirty pages, filled with elaborate illustrations photocopied from books and page after page of photocopied score. Producing an impressive handout is not the same as preparing an effective presentation; in fact, if all your time goes into gathering materials, the presentation itself will almost certainly be ill-prepared and ineffective. It is extremely costly and probably illegal to make multiple copies of large sections of scores or movements. Be as selective with musical examples as you are with recorded examples; you can probably illustrate any stylistic point you wish to make by including a few short musical examples or by creating your own diagrams or graphics to illustrate large-scale organization or structure. At the other extreme, some students distribute handouts that are not very helpful—perhaps a hastily assembled bibliography in desperate need of editing and proofreading. Anything you distribute with your name on it should be put together and edited with the same care you would use on a research paper.

There are other ways besides handouts to provide scores for the class; one alternative is to bring multiple copies of the appropriate scores. If you choose this method, think carefully about the logistics and keep the time constraints in mind. If the scores are different editions with different page numbers, or if some students will be reading a piano-vocal score and others an orchestral score, the members of the class may spend all their time trying to figure out where they are supposed to be in the scores. If your plan calls for the group to look at several short examples from different collections, the whole presentation can turn into a complicated and distracting exercise in circulating and collecting scores, and no one will hear what you have to say. Once an important point is made clear through close reading of one selected score example, it may be better to have the class listen to other recorded examples rather than try to provide a score for each recorded example. After all, music majors should be able to listen analytically and make stylistic judgments by ear, particularly after their attention has been drawn to the point you are trying to illustrate. Difficult choices have to be made, just as they do in a paper; every example, whether it is a page from a score, a diagram, or a recorded example, must clearly support the point you are trying to make.

Once you have your outline, your plans for the handout, and your recorded examples clearly in mind, if you still have doubts about whether your choices are realistic, you may want to consult your instructor for a preliminary reaction. This strategy is especially appropriate for the student whose presentation is scheduled first; the person in this position is at a disadvantage, because there are no prior models to serve as guides. If you consult your instructor, he or she will probably be willing to tell you whether your plans seem realistic and whether it is likely that you can accomplish what you intend to accomplish in the time allotted.

Multimedia presentations   Students who have the ability and the equipment to produce multimedia presentations should consider using multimedia tools to enhance their presentations. At the simplest level, one might show a few slides of helpful illustrations. Other students might want to experiment with PowerPoint presentations incorporating audio and video clips. Working out an impressive presentation, however, should not occupy all the presenter's time and effort; the multimedia resources should be used only to enhance the student's solid research and careful organization of the material.

Tone and Approach

Finally, as you prepare your outline, handout, and examples, and as the time for your presentation gets closer, think about the impression you want to create. Imagine yourself standing in front of the group, and think about your own experience sitting in class over the years; you know exactly the sort of approach that appeals to you and the approaches that offend you or put you to sleep. Remember that audiences generally come to a lecture or presentation with an interest in the topic and a willingness to listen. As long as speakers appear to know what they are talking about, are well prepared, and are enthusiastic about communicating their insights, you will listen. Your willingness to listen will last through the whole presentation, unless the speaker interferes with your interest by appearing unprepared or uninterested. To hold the attention of a class, one need not be a superb public speaker. Think about your favorite professors over the years. I would bet that the good ones stand out in your mind because they knew and loved the material and communicated it clearly and effectively, not because they were great orators.

You want to communicate to your audience that you know what you are doing, are interested in your topic, have spent considerable time in research, and will move crisply through your outline. Walk up to the platform the way you walk out on stage for a performance, looking as assured as you can, not as if you were heading to the dentist for root canal work or to the IRS office to have your tax return audited. You should assume that the audience is interested in your topic and make clear by your look and behavior that you will not waste their precious time. Think of yourself as a competent professional; you stand before your colleagues not as a preacher exhorting them to some action or as an entertainer trying to amuse them. You are there as a researcher reporting on the insights and knowledge you have gained, sharing with them your vision of some specific musical works or historical developments. If you have done the necessary research and planned your presentation carefully, and if you present yourself in this way, the experience will be surprisingly satisfying, both for you and for your audience.

CONCERT REPORTS

Another type of assignment that involves writing about music is the concert report. Generally, when professors assign reports, they make clear exactly what they expect the students to do, but there are a few useful generalizations we can make about this kind of assignment.

Purpose

Although each instructor may have his or her own goals in assigning concert reports, most see these reports primarily as extensions of the class-room discussions. Concert reports are an example of what psychologists call second-order learning—applying newly acquired conceptual information and insight to new experiences. It is one thing to absorb what an instructor says in class and be able to repeat it in an examination; it is another thing altogether to have such command of the analytical methods and stylistic in-sights discussed in class that you can apply them as a means of understand-ing new musical experiences.

The focus of a concert report should therefore be on the music and mu-sical style. Too many concert reports, whether they are written by students in a music appreciation class or by music majors, waste a great deal of time discussing issues that have nothing to do with musical style—descriptions of the hall, the audience, or what the performers were wearing, or the writer's evaluation of the quality of the performance. A concert report is different from music criticism, which is a form of journalism. Although questions of performance practice may be relevant to your discussion of musical style, discussion of the quality of the performance can too easily degenerate into negative criticism of the playing or comments about problems of ensemble coordination, intonation, and the like. I have even read concert reports that opened with complaints about how hard it was to find the concert venue or a convenient parking space. My response is simple: Get over it, and tell me about the music.

What instructors want to see in concert reports is discussion of the music that was performed, especially if the student can connect it with pieces and issues discussed in class. Classes studying early music, for exam-ple, are frequently asked to attend concerts of music composed before 1750 and relate what they hear to the stylistic developments discussed in class. Comparisons to specific works discussed in class are always welcome. Dis-cussion of performance practice issues is also welcome; instructors expect that the students will apply the information they have learned in class to all musical experiences in the future. If the report is an assignment in a music appreciation class, students should apply their newly acquired knowledge about the elements of music—rhythm, texture, color, harmony, and so forth—to the music they heard.

Research

It sometimes surprises students to find out that they might have to do some research before attending a concert and writing a report on it. Con-certgoers who are already armed with an understanding of the history, back-ground, and style or structure of a particular work will be in a much better position to discuss the work from a stylistic viewpoint and to judge whether the performance was stylistically valid than those who are unprepared. It is lack of preparation, or lack of advance understanding of what a work is about, that leads desperate students to resort to simply repeating the commentary that appears in the program notes or discussing irrelevancies such as the dress or behavior of the audience. I should add that copying the printed program notes instead of writing about your own ideas and reactions is another example of plagiarism, and is probably copyright infringement as well. If discovered, this behavior could result in a failing grade for the course and a hearing before the committee on student conduct.

Writing the Report

Students often wonder how to begin writing a concert report. The opening paragraphs should provide the basic information about the concert—who, what, where, when. Who were the performers—a professional orchestra, a student ensemble, a chamber group, a soloist? Did the group include unusual instruments, or the standard ones for that type of ensemble? What works were performed? After providing that basic information, decide which works you want to discuss in detail—perhaps the pieces that relate most closely to the class, or the ones you found most interesting. It may be possible to focus most of your attention on one work, the one closest to the material of recent class discussions, and summarize the rest of the concert in a sentence or two. In discussing the music, use the analytic categories and the technical vocabulary that you use in class. Obviously, one expects more technical detail about issues such as structure, harmony, and orchestration from music majors than from nonmajors, but both groups should be able to use what they are learning in class in their discussions of the concerts they attend. Music majors might compare their expectations before the concert with what they actually heard. Were there surprising or unique elements in any of the pieces, or did the music stay close to what the informed listener would expect? Did the live performance help to underline some things about the music that one would not be able to observe in the same way from a recording? Preparation, sensitive listening, and imagination will lead you to choose the best direction for your discussion.

As you draft your concert report, always keep musical style foremost in your mind. Focusing on stylistic issues will demonstrate to your instructor that you have thought about class discussions and that you can handle stylistic questions competently and intelligently. An informed, focused, and thoughtful report that grapples with musical issues will be a success.

Finally, a word of caution. Students, particularly those who are not music majors, are often not aware that putting on a recital or a concert is a very difficult enterprise, and that problems can arise at the last minute. Performers get sick, a difficult piece just doesn't come together in the available rehearsal time, the performers decide at the last minute that changing the order of the pieces on the program would make a more unified or more logically organized performance, and so forth. Even professional recitals and concerts change at the last minute; pieces are substituted, the order is changed, or the artists perform an encore or two after the official program is over. Since the printed program naturally has to be produced in advance, it may not represent exactly what was actually played at the performance. You can see where this is going; students sometimes pick up a program, assume it will be followed exactly, and then go home to write up their concert reports without staying to hear the concert. It is not even safe to leave at intermission, if there is one; changes can happen in the second half. I have read glowing accounts of performances that never happened, because the pieces were cancelled or changed at the last minute. Even if your instructor or teaching assistant does not attend the concert, other students who stayed for the concert will report on the changes in the program, and what you thought was a slick strategy can leave you in serious trouble. Go to the concert or recital, listen carefully, take some notes, and report on what you actually heard and how it relates to material discussed in class.

PROGRAM NOTES

At some point during your life as a student or later in the professional world, you will probably be asked to write program notes for a recital or a concert. Program notes present a special challenge to the writer because of their special purpose and because of the severe space limitations that are usually imposed.

Purpose

Program notes are different from research papers. Papers are written to demonstrate competence in research and scholarship and therefore must include the standard scholarly apparatus of footnotes and bibliography. The purpose of program notes, on the other hand, is not primarily scholarship, although whatever you write must be based on solid research and analysis. The purpose of program notes is to increase the audience members' understanding of the music to be performed and therefore their enjoyment of the concert. If listeners have the opportunity in advance to learn something about the background of the piece, its special purpose, or the ways in which it is unique, they have something specific to listen for and are less likely to sit passively, letting the music wash over them. Intelligent listeners appreciate informative, well-written program notes.

Who Is the Audience?

It is often difficult to gauge the background and knowledge an audience brings to a concert; it is therefore difficult to estimate the level of technical knowledge you can assume in your writing. Avoid overly technical analysis that will make no sense to the majority of the audience. Conversely, do not insult the audience's intelligence by assuming that they know nothing at all about music. Obviously, people who devote their valuable time and money to attending concerts already have an interest in music. Most members of concert audiences collect classical recordings and have a fair general knowledge of the history of music. Write for an imaginary nonmusician who is interested in music and is fairly well read. If the program consists of standard works, your imaginary reader probably already knows something about them and probably has heard other live or recorded performances of these pieces. This imaginary listener still appreciates being reminded, or told for the first time, about the special circumstances surrounding the composition of a particular work, the composer's intent, and what makes the work unique.

Writing for a particular audience may be especially troublesome when the program notes are for a recital presented as part of your work toward a degree. The audience will probably include relatives and friends who are there mainly because they are proud of you, not because they have any special interest in the pieces you will play; teachers, who will judge the recital on technical grounds; and your student colleagues, who will bring their special knowledge and background to the experience. In that situation, do not try to write for your relatives or for your teachers; instead, write for your colleagues, who are somewhere in the middle between these two extremes. Try to write at a more technical level than would be appropriate for a general concert audience, but do not assume that everyone knows the music as intimately as you and your teacher do.

Research

Approach the research for program notes in the same way you approach research for a paper, using the same resources and methodology, beginning with dictionaries and encyclopedias, histories, biographies, and thematic catalogs. It may seem strange to pursue the same sort of research to write a few short paragraphs of program notes as you would for a twenty-page paper, but whatever you write in program notes, no matter how brief, must be based on a thorough understanding of the music, as well as awareness of the background of the work, where it fits in the composer's output, and the composer's intent. In writing program notes, one rarely uses all the information uncovered in one's research, but it is a serious mistake to toss off a few casual comments. If you are going to perform the work you are writing about, you should have analyzed it already, but you may need to do some research on its background and on the composer's intent. If you do not already know the work thoroughly, that must be the first step in your research—no one should ever write about a musical work without studying the score and hearing a recording, if possible. The audience may not realize that the few paragraphs they read are based on hours of careful research, but each sentence you write must be based on thorough knowledge. The world does not need any more vague, fanciful, or flowery program notes; quite enough of that sort of prose has been written already. The process of research into musical topics is explained in Chapter 3.

Working within Limits

The main constraint on program notes is always limited space. If you are told that there is room in the program for five hundred words, then you must stay within that limit. If you go over the word limit, you cause endless problems for the people responsible for printing the program. If there is time, they might ask you to shorten your prose, or else they will do it themselves; they might even leave out the notes altogether. If your limit is five hundred words, then everything you say must fit on somewhat less than two pages of double-spaced typescript with normal margins. Every word you write must be carefully chosen. Space limitations are not always that severe, but the writer must always stay within whatever limit is imposed.

In some ways it is more difficult to discuss a piece of music in a paragraph or two than to write a twenty-page paper about it. In a paper, one has the leisure to develop ideas at some length, cite long quotations, and write extended analytical discussions. There is no room in program notes for footnotes; quotations must be brief and be chosen with great care. It can be very helpful to quote a composer's words about what he had in mind for a particular work, but all quotations must be short and effective. One usually cannot include musical examples, and extended analyses are impossible because of the space limitations. Besides, program notes in the "then this happens, then this happens" style make dull reading. The writer hopes to draw the listener's attention to something interesting or unique about a particular work; frequently, that is all one can accomplish. Program notes are not research papers, but neither are they collections of vague sentiments about music in general or about a particular composer. Through a kind of sleight of hand, the writer tries to convey a genuine understanding of a particular work in a few well-chosen words.

As you can see, it is a challenging task to write effective program notes. Sometimes, in an attempt to meet a deadline, one is tempted to simply copy or paraphrase material from published collections of program notes or from the notes that accompany a recording. Needless to say, such copying constitutes plagiarism, an illegal act in both the academic world and the publishing world, and a serious mistake, just as it would be in a paper. Some published notes and CD booklets are written in a flowery style that would be difficult to pass off as your own work, and some have little worthwhile to say about the music. It is clearly better to do your own research, study the music, and try to communicate your insight in a clear and informative manner in the short space allotted to you.

Special Problems

Some kinds of concerts present special challenges for the writer of program notes. The following brief comments offer general guidelines for writing program notes in these special situations.

Early music   The music of the medieval, Renaissance, and Baroque periods was usually written to be performed in a context far different from today's concert hall. Early music, at least that portion that was written down, was generally performed either in church or in court. Composers and performers worked for the church or the aristocracy and succeeded as long as they continued to provide the kind of music that would satisfy their powerful patrons.

It is often helpful for the audience to be reminded of the special circumstances for which a work was written. Think, for example, of the pieces discussed in Chapter 2. Listeners would be better prepared to appreciate a performance of Dufay's *Nuper rosarum flores* if they understood something of the special circumstances surrounding its purpose and performance. Even if a listener cannot hear the mathematical relationships between the two slow-moving lines, it is helpful to know that Dufay was trying to model his musical structures on the architectural proportions of the new dome. At a concert performance of a Bach cantata, the audience should understand that the cantatas were not written as concert pieces, but were part of the long Sunday morning service of the German Lutheran church, a way to illuminate the message of that particular day's Gospel reading.

There are other historical questions that may deserve comment. In the Middle Ages and the Renaissance, and to some extent in the Baroque period, composer and performer were the same person, not two different specialists. Music was often written for instruments and vocal groups different from the ones that usually perform the music now. In addition, most early music was written in a shorthand form, so that performers must reconstruct the musical details rather than following specific directions set down by the composer. The audience should understand these historical differences in the fundamental relationship between composer and performer, and should be aware of the decisions for which the performers are responsible, as well as the circumstances for which the music was originally written. If modern instruments are substituted for the instruments that the composer intended, that fact should be noted. One need not construct an elaborate defense of the practice, but neither should the writer pretend that the composer wrote these works for modern instruments. If pianists want to perform Bach on twelve-foot Steinways, they have a perfect right to do so, provided they understand something of Baroque style, but the listener should be aware that Bach wrote for a different instrument altogether and that using modern instruments may alter the sound the composer had in mind. If large choruses choose to perform sixteenth-century madrigals, listeners should be aware that these pieces were originally written for chamber vocal groups with one voice on each part and performed in much more intimate venues than the modern concert hall. Whatever the writer can convey about the original purpose and sound of the music will help the audience appreciate the performance better and will equip them to make an intelligent judgment about the success of the performers' reconstructive work.

Transcriptions, arrangements, and editions　　An allied issue is the relationship between what the performers play and what the composer actually wrote. Listeners should be told something of the history of a work if they are to appreciate the performance. If a particular clavier concerto by Bach, for example, is a transcription of a violin concerto by Vivaldi, the notes should mention that fact. If the score used in a performance is a modern transcription or arrangement of an earlier work, that fact should also be noted. Another example from the music of Bach comes to mind. Cellists enjoy performing the so-called gamba sonatas of Bach; these works, however, were transcribed by Bach for solo gamba and harpsichord with an obbligato right-hand part from earlier trio sonatas written for two treble instruments and continuo, in which the harpsichord part consists of a figured bass line and an improvised part for the right hand. Again, this information is interesting to the intelligent listener. In the same way, modern editions or restorations of the original versions of works from the Romantic period, or from any period, should be noted. Reminding an audience that, for example, they will hear the chamber orchestra version of Copland's *Appalachian Spring* should focus their listening and make them think about the differences between that version and the more familiar version for full orchestra. The audience certainly wants to know whether what they hear is the original work, a version "corrected" by an editor, or a modern reconstruction of the original version.

Recent music　　World premieres and recently composed music can pose problems for the writer of program notes. The usual research resources are of limited use; lexicons and books on twentieth-century music may contain useful information about the lives of composers and their place in twentieth-century music, but not about recently composed works. If you are writing the notes for your own performance, you can work from your knowledge of the score; if not, it may be difficult to gain access to a score. In that case, you may have to contact the composer or some other knowledgeable person—a performer or a concert presenter who knows the work— by mail or in person. Some composers are very helpful in explaining the genesis and the structure of their works; others dislike discussing their creations and prefer to let their works speak for them. I have heard composers, when asked about their works, embark on long disquisitions about Oriental philosophy, higher mathematics, or antiwar sentiments. Still, the diligent investigator can usually find out something of what the composer had in mind and where the work fits in the evolution of twentieth-century musical styles. Any information of this sort is helpful to the listener, who then is saved from the danger of judging the work against the wrong set of expectations. The composer's ideas may or may not be audible in the performance, but at least the listener knows what to listen for and can judge whether the work communicates what the composer had in mind.

Familiar repertory   The writer faces the opposite problem when writing program notes about works everyone knows, such as the Beethoven symphonies or some of the better-known late Romantic works. One feels tongue-tied and a bit foolish when trying to write about these works; what can there be left to say about the *Eroica,* for example, or the Chopin preludes? The way to approach this situation is exactly the way one approaches any writing about music—research. One can always discuss basic issues such as the background of the work, the composer's intent, the structure of the work, or the qualities that make it unique. Vast amounts of information have been written about the better-known composers and their works, so that in one sense it is easier to find things to say. Published letters of composers may contain information about what the composer thought of the work, the circumstances of the first performance, and the reaction of the audience and the critics. It is easy to find the writings of well-known composers; a carefully chosen quotation may give the reader a new slant on a familiar work.

Texts and Translations

One final issue that should be discussed is that of providing texts and translations of vocal music. In general, listeners should always be provided with the text, whether the singers will be singing in English or in a foreign language. If the performance will be in a foreign language, listeners should have at hand both the original text and an English translation so that they can follow the text as it is performed and can consult the translation in case they do not read the foreign language with facility.

The principle is clear enough, but some situations present special problems. If a text is extremely long or if there are multiple texts, as in a *Lieder* recital, reprinting both texts and translations may take a large amount of space. In that case, a separate insert containing the texts and translations can be folded into the program. Some texts are familiar to most listeners; if a choral group is performing a Renaissance setting of the Ordinary of the Mass, for example, most members of the audience would know the familiar liturgical texts and what they mean in English. Even in that case, however, programs frequently contain both text and translation. If you have a choice, always choose the most literal translation rather than the most beautiful English version; when the translation stays close to the original word order, the members of the audience are in a better position to judge the aptness of the musical setting to the individual words of text. If the translator's name is known, it should always be included with the translation. Remember also that it is illegal to reprint a published translation without permission. Finally, when you have gone to the trouble of providing texts and translations, make sure there is enough light in the hall for the audience to read them during the performance. It makes little sense to provide texts and then turn the houselights down so far that the hall is too dark for reading.

Conclusion

Writing program notes can be a daunting challenge because of the severe space limitations and the special problems posed by some kinds of repertory. Informative and carefully written program notes, however, are welcomed by intelligent audience members and can add greatly to the listening experience and therefore the success of the concert.

ESSAY EXAMINATIONS

There is another type of writing about music that is very much part of your life as a student—answering essay questions about music in examinations. As you can imagine, reading a large number of essay questions can be a discouraging task; few people can produce effective prose under the pressure that surrounds an examination. The answers usually vary enormously in quality, from unorganized facts scrawled in incomplete and awkward sentences to the occasional well-organized and convincing essay. Knowing how to approach essay questions can materially affect your examination grades and therefore your academic success. This section discusses the purpose of essay questions, how to prepare for them, the steps to follow in writing a successful essay as part of an examination, and some common errors students fall into in this type of examination.

Purpose

Professors do not include essay questions in their examinations just to be cruel or because they have a deep-seated compulsion to read vast quantities of bad prose. Essay questions are important because they are the only way students can demonstrate their grasp of important material, and because they call for insight, understanding, and the ability to synthesize large amounts of information and focus on what is most significant. After all, neither art nor life is multiple-choice. For a professor to ask only objective or short-answer questions is to do injustice to the material covered, since the history of music is much more than a series of unrelated factoids. Essay questions are the only way to test the student's grasp of the big picture, as well as important trends and connections.

Preparing for Essay Examinations

One of the important advantages of essay questions, from the instructor's point of view, is that preparing for them can give shape and coherence to the process of reviewing the material. Studying for the examination thus becomes an important and useful part of the learning experience, not simply an exercise in memorizing facts.

There are several steps involved in preparing for essay questions. First, find out in advance whether there will be essay questions on the examination, and if so, how many there are likely to be. Once you find out that there will be essay questions, make a list of those areas you judge to be particularly important, the material that was given special emphasis by the instructor. If you pick out four or five areas that you think are obvious choices for essay questions, you can be fairly sure that one or more of them will appear in some form on the examination. You have survived examinations in the past, and you know how they work. Professors naturally give special emphasis to those areas they think are particularly important, and they know it would be pointless to ask essay questions about side issues or unimportant details. Assume that your professor is a reasonable and logical person, even when making up examination questions. If you go over your notes with an eye to what the professor emphasized, you can figure out what the questions will be and plan your answers. You can even design outlines for the answers to the questions you think are most likely to appear on the examination so that your answers will be logical, coherent, and organized. If you go about preparing in the right way, there is no reason why you should be surprised by the questions your professor chooses. It seems so simple; here is a legal way to find out about the examination questions in advance.

How to Proceed

Before you start writing your answer to an essay question, pause and think. That is not an easy thing to do; students usually approach examinations in a state of nervousness, their minds crammed with recently reviewed facts, pencils poised to write as much as possible as quickly as possible before all the information flies out of their heads. Working quickly and impulsively is usually not a bad strategy, and is probably the best way to approach objective questions, but it is not the way to answer essay questions.

First, read the question a second time to be sure you understand it. Ask the instructor if you are not sure what the question means. Look for key words. Does the question ask you to *outline* the important stages in the evolution of a particular style, to *discuss* a particular work or a particular artistic movement, or to *compare and contrast* two works, styles, or composers? There are only a few kinds of essay questions, and professors try very hard to frame their questions as clearly as possible. Pause and think about the question. What is included? What is not? Are there terms that need to be defined as the first step? Does the question set limits?

Next, outline your answer and tinker with the outline for a while. Maybe your answer would make better sense if you changed the order of ideas, or perhaps there is something in your outline that you are prepared to discuss but does not really fit with the question. Accept the fact that you may not get a chance to demonstrate every little bit of your recently acquired knowledge. It is better to answer the question briefly and stay on the point than to write three pages of brilliant prose about some other topic.

After you are satisfied that your outline adequately covers the area specified by the question and that you have not left out anything important or included something irrelevant, start writing your answer. If there is time, write a rough draft and edit it before you copy your final version. Stay on the point, and force yourself to follow your outline. Avoid the tendency to spew out unrelated facts, and do your best to produce a piece of writing that flows logically and coherently. Finally, assuming there is still time, edit and proofread your answer, make sure it is legible, and delete anything that is ungrammatical, incoherent, or not relevant to the question. Remember that your aim is to demonstrate understanding, insight, and the ability to organize information, not to produce a long list of unrelated facts. Remember also that your professor will have to read a large stack of examinations. Imagine what a pleasure it is for him or her to encounter a clearly organized, carefully written essay. Even if two different answers contain the same information, the one that is a coherent and careful piece of writing will be more successful than a rambling, disorganized scrawl. The trick is to organize the information, not just regurgitate it.

Common Errors

The common mistakes that students make when writing essay examinations are easily avoidable. The greatest mistake is not reading the question and the instructions carefully. Some students pounce on a key word that triggers a flood of facts, without first asking which facts are relevant. When asked, for example, to contrast impressionism and neoclassicism in the twentieth century, some students see only the word "impressionism" and launch into a description of Debussy's life and career, without stopping to realize that that is not what the question is about. Focus on exactly what the question asks for. If the question is "Trace the evolution of the motet from Notre Dame polyphony through the French Ars Nova," do not write about the English school, no matter how thoroughly you have reviewed Dunstable's motets. If the question is "Discuss *The Rake's Progress* as an example of Stravinsky's neoclassical style," do not ramble on about the Octet for Winds, even if you have played it and know it much better than you know *The Rake*. Even if you are convinced that the octet is a better example of neoclassicism than the opera, you still have to write about *The Rake's Progress*. Although it seems obvious that the key to success is to answer the question posed by the instructor rather than choosing a topic you like better, time and again students wander off into areas specifically excluded by the professor's carefully written questions.

Another major mistake in writing essay questions is to spew out an unorganized jumble of facts more or less related to the question, rather than a thoughtful, coherent essay. Many students seem to think that their task is to write everything they can think of, a sort of stew filled with nuggets of unrelated information, leaving it to the instructor to pick out whatever he or she wants. All the important facts are in there somewhere, if the instructor is willing to dredge for them and does not care about the order in which things appear. When asked to compare and contrast two schools or styles, for example, some students write separate, detailed descriptions of the two styles, never addressing the question of specific ways in which they are similar or different. That approach is distressingly common; it may be a result of the overemphasis on isolated facts in some music history books, as well as in our educational system in general. Some blame this tendency on the television age, with its emphasis on sound bites and short bursts of information, or on the nervousness with which students approach examinations. Never underestimate the importance of logical organization and coherence. If you read the question carefully, stay on the point, and try to write decent prose, you will succeed—it's that simple.

Another common error is careless use of technical terms. In their haste, some students mix up important technical terms and thus make it hard for the reader to know what they are trying to say. An examination is not the place to throw around technical terms loosely; a mistake like that can ruin what otherwise might be a fine answer. Chapter 8 has a section on proper use of technical terms; review that section with the examination situation in mind.

The last common error is failing to proofread and edit your essay. Your professor has no way of knowing how well you have answered the question if your answer is an illegible mess. See that your comments are legible, correct as many misspellings and grammatical errors as you can in the remaining time, copy the essay over if it needs it, and make the essay look as competent and professional as you can, granting the pressures of the examination situation.

To summarize, remember that the object of essay questions is not to produce a reflex response or some isolated bits of information, but to demonstrate your mastery of the topic and your ability to select the most significant events and trends relevant to the question and organize your ideas in a logical and convincing fashion. Essay questions are a test of understanding and insight, not a test of whether you have memorized an impressive list of bits of information. Logic, coherence, and clear writing will be much more successful than several pages of hastily scrawled facts.

CONCLUSION

Besides the projects discussed in this chapter, there are still other kinds of writing projects that challenge music students. The lecture-recital, for instance, is an especially daunting challenge, combining a kind of seminar presentation with a public performance. I did not discuss lecture-recitals in this chapter because in my experience they are not likely to be required of undergraduate majors. However, you can imagine what the lecture part of the event would require—extensive research, careful writing and editing, and consideration of things like slides or handouts to help present your ideas effectively.

As you reflect on the kinds of projects discussed in this chapter, note that, different as the challenges are in these various activities, there are important common elements in writing a paper, giving a seminar presentation, writing a concert report, writing program notes, and writing an essay in an examination. There are two basic concepts that will guide you successfully through any of these challenges. The first is research. No one, whoever the writer is and whatever the context is, should ever write or speak about music without being solidly grounded in creative and thorough research. Even a fifteen-minute presentation or brief program notes should be based on extensive research. The second requirement in all these situations is a professional attitude toward preparing and presenting your ideas.

CHAPTER 7

Writing Style

Chapters 7 and 8 present some basic ideas about writing effective prose. Since most students passed a writing course early in their college careers, much of this material will probably serve as a review rather than new information. Many books on writing treat these matters in much more detail; this section is intended only as a brief guide, included here for your convenience. Although much of this discussion applies to any expository writing, it also includes some issues peculiar to papers on musical topics. This chapter will review some general principles and details of effective writing style; Chapter 8 will discuss common writing problems that detract from the effectiveness of student papers.

SOME BASIC IDEAS ABOUT WRITING

After reading hundreds of student papers as well as producing various kinds of writing myself, including articles for scholarly journals, textbooks, and program notes, I have become convinced of some basic truths about writing.

1. *Effective writing is a learned skill, not an inborn talent.* It is frustrating to hear students say "I just don't write very well," or "I've always been a poor speller," with a shrug, as if this lack of skill were an endearing imperfection over which they had no control. The ability to spell correctly or write well is not something genetic; it is a skill we learn and refine through years of effort. Writing convincing, effective prose is work; there is no particular mystique about it, and it is not a kind of magical power conferred on a few lucky persons. Anyone willing to work at it can learn to write clearly and forcefully.

2. *We all can improve our writing skills.* Assuming that you have the basic skills for writing English prose, you do not need special courses, tutors,

or technical training to hone those skills. Naturally, if English is your second language and you have difficulty speaking and writing it correctly, you may need the help of special courses and tutors. Most students have some writing skills; what they need is to improve them. We all can improve our writing. Even prominent scholars and writers sometimes produce prose that is less than perfect; much of the material we read each day could be improved by further revising and editing. Good writers work harder than you might imagine to make the words say exactly what they want to say, and they constantly strive to improve their writing style. Read about Ernest Hemingway and the way he worked. He is famous for editing and cutting his drafts ruthlessly, until the final version was one-fourth the size of his original draft, or less, and the words were finally distilled down to the lean, direct style that is the hallmark of his writing.

3. *Music students should think of their papers as a kind of performance and try to attain the same professional standard in their writing as they do in their performances.* If you expect your ideas and insights to be taken seriously, you must learn how to communicate them effectively in a carefully written and edited paper. I am amazed that the same students who present themselves as consummate professionals in their performances sometimes tolerate low standards in their academic work. Imagine what their recitals would be like if they prepared and presented them with the same casual attitude that sometimes mars their written assignments. Unkempt performers would wander onto the stage a half-hour late, stumble through a slapdash performance, and then feign shock when their teachers disapproved. Recitals like that never happen, because students understand the high standards expected of them in performance. Extend those same professional standards to your written work.

4. *There are different types of writing, each with its own standards and rules.* What might be perfectly appropriate in poetry, fiction, or personal letters may not be suitable in a research paper. One brief example will suffice to illustrate this idea. In a love poem by e. e. cummings (he insisted on the lowercase initials), there is a memorable line: "If a look should April me . . ." Turning the name of a month associated with spring, melting snow, soft rains, and new life into a verb is a wonderfully expressive poetic device, an example of the creativity and the flair for striking language that we expect of poets. That same device, however, would be completely out of place in a research paper. Research papers are regarded as expository prose, as opposed to journalism, poetry, or fiction, and the overriding goal of expository prose is clarity and persuasiveness, not the startling and allusive use of language that creates poetry. Expository prose is not the demanding art that poetry is; anyone can learn and apply the standards of expository prose.

5. *There are specific steps you can take to improve your writing.* First, read. Read all sorts of writing—novels, mysteries, short stories, essays, histories,

biographies. Don't confine your reading to what is required for class; turn off the television and the computer and read for pleasure when you have a spare moment. Read critically, with an eye to appreciating good style. Second, write. The only way to learn how to write better is to write and rewrite. Write a draft, then revise, edit, cut, polish, get opinions from reliable critics, and continue rewriting. There are no shortcuts to producing a first-quality paper, any more than there are shortcuts to a good performance.

KINDS OF PROSE

Expository prose is different from much of the writing we see each day, because it is designed to inform and explain. Other kinds of writing have different purposes. Advertising copy, for example, is often designed not so much to convey information as to create an aura of pleasant associations around a product; the prose frequently speaks to our emotions rather than to our minds. Think about the way cars are advertised on television. Some ads do not even mention equipment, horsepower, or safety features. Instead, the words and pictures are designed to make us feel good about the car or convince us that we would feel better about ourselves if we owned that car. You notice that the people in automobile ads never use their shiny cars to drop off the kids at school, return a video, or run to the grocery store for supplies. They never get caught on a crowded freeway or even drive on city streets; the cars are always speeding along empty roads in the Colorado Rockies or through a picturesque desert somewhere in New Mexico. The ads don't highlight facts; they promise freedom and the wind in your hair. Look closely at the men in most beer ads. They are never accountants or salesmen or algebra teachers, and certainly not music students; they are always deep-sea fishermen, steelworkers, or construction workers, real he-men who go for the gusto and like their pleasures big and brawny. The implication is that we would be like them if we only drank the right beer. The ads are about feelings, not facts. Similarly, a person looking for a home to purchase quickly learns how to translate the special language of real estate ads. "Needs a little love" means that it will probably cost $30,000 in repairs to keep the place standing for a few more years, and "cute" usually means the space is unbelievably tiny.

   Just as advertising prose is designed to create appealing associations around a product, prose can be written to mask or sanitize unpleasant ideas, through what is called *euphemism*. When politicians speak of "revenue enhancement strategies" instead of "raising taxes," they are trying to hide the real meaning from suspicious voters. Politicians refer to social programs run by religious organizations as "faith-based programs," avoiding the word "church," trying to forestall any outcry about the separation of church and state. The military is particularly expert at creating euphemisms; "friendly fire" and "collateral damage" are startling examples of neutral, pleasant-sounding terms for ugly realities. Another fine example came from the space program; after the space shuttle *Challenger* tragically exploded in midair, a NASA spokesman referred to the remains of those killed in the explosion as "recovered components" and called the boxes in which those remains were shipped home "crew transfer containers."

Frequently, prose is designed to make the writer look important rather than to explain ideas. When academic committees speak of "curriculum evaluation criteria" or "recruitment strategies for the modern multiversity," are they really discussing ideas, or are they trying to sound important and powerful? When a businessman speaks of "ballpark projections on the downside effects of targeting our marketing to new demographics," he too is playing a role, creating an impression, announcing to the world that he is a hardheaded, sophisticated business expert. Note the sports jargon—numbers are "ballpark figures," not "estimates." Some business types like to pepper their comments with sports jargon—"slam dunk," "full-court press," "third and long," "step up to the plate," "home run." Whereas businessmen use the language of professional sports, educators talk like businessmen. University administrators have adopted both the thinking and the jargon of the business world, saying things like "using our Web site to build brand recognition," "selling our program in a whole new market," and even adopting the business world's strange-sounding new cliché, "growing our program." Keep your ears attuned to the words that surround us. Language is endlessly fascinating, and it is employed in the pursuit of many different goals; straightforward transmission and explanation of ideas is only one of its uses.

Read the prose that comes your way with a critical eye, listen to the ads on television, and ask yourself what the writer's purpose is and how it is achieved. Once you begin to understand the manifold ways in which words can be used, the purpose of expository prose should be clearer as well, and you will better understand the tone and style appropriate for it.

TONE

Since the purpose of expository prose is to inform and explain, its main goal is clarity. Your goal in a paper about music is to convey ideas and insight about a complicated art as clearly and directly as possible. The focus should be on communicating concepts, not on making yourself sound important. Your prose should be as direct and as simple as you can make it, so that the reader will be informed and enlightened. The tone of your writing should be crisp, professional, and businesslike. That is not to say that you should avoid using technical terms. Like the jargon of all fields, the technical terms of music exist because we need them. There is no other economical way to communicate complex concepts like "fugue" or "sonata-allegro structure"; the technical terms convey precise information to the musically informed reader. As to the rest of your language, however, clarity and crispness of expression are the goals.

Two extremes are to be avoided. Expository prose is different from speech and informal writing, such as personal letters. A slangy or cute tone is therefore completely out of place in a formal paper. Sometimes student papers contain sentences like "I was bummed when I discovered that . . ." or "The tenor is all 'I love you,' but the soprano is all 'No way.'" Such casual language is inappropriate in a research paper. Sometimes students place quotation marks around words they know are questionable, as if that somehow absolves them from responsibility. Putting quotation marks around "bummed," for example, does not exonerate the writer from the charge of poor word choice. In fact, it compounds the problem, because now there is the additional error of using quotation marks where there is no valid reason for them.

It is more common for student writers to go to the other extreme and adopt a stilted, artificial style, perhaps because they were taught to use overly formal language in their papers or because they feel that such a style creates an impression of serious scholarship. One frequently sees awkward, impersonal constructions like "It has long been assumed that . . ." and "The present writer finds it well-nigh impossible to agree with this position." Sometimes the writing becomes overly flowery and dramatic, as in the following example.

> When Josquin entered the service of the Duke as a young choirboy, little did the world suspect that in the future he would have such a profound impact, not only on the history of music, but on all of Western culture.

You see the problem—that sentence should be accompanied by a dramatic drumroll. The proper tone for expository writing is somewhere between these two extremes. The first priority should always be clarity. Individual concepts must be explained as clearly as possible, ideas must be set forth in a unified and coherent way, and the argument must flow logically so that the reader can follow it. Your writing should be clear, crisp, economical, businesslike, and professional.

THE STANCE OF THE WRITER

Related to the question of tone is the issue of the writer's stance, or how involved the person of the writer should be in the prose. Again, there are two extremes to avoid. At one extreme is the intrusive writer. Some students write with a tone of breathless discovery, as if no one had ever considered these ideas or heard this music before. This approach tells the reader more about the naiveté of the inexperienced researcher than about the topic.

At the other extreme is the elusive or invisible writer. As I explained earlier, research means more than merely reporting the ideas of others. As a researcher, you are expected to design a thesis and argue it by studying the evidence, reviewing the secondary literature, analyzing the music, and forming your own conclusions, based on your analytical ability and critical judgment. As you write about your research, you are expected to take a stand and communicate your opinions. After the writer cites expert A and expert B, the reader waits for the other shoe to drop—what does the writer think? To stay aloof from your prose, reluctant to get involved and take a stand, is to shirk one of the fundamental responsibilities of the researcher.

REFERRING TO YOURSELF

The question of the writer's stance brings up the question of how you should refer to yourself in your prose. Many of us were trained to avoid the first-person pronoun in our writing and find it difficult to write the word "I" in a paper. Most instructors now agree that "I" is perfectly acceptable, provided that it is used with restraint and reserved for those moments when the writer is sharing his or her own thoughts. Clearly, "I" is out of place when discussing someone else's ideas, but there are few alternatives to "I" when it comes to the writer's own conclusions. "The present writer" is an awkward and distracting phrase. "I" seems much more natural in a sentence like "A says this and B says that; I agree with B." One can, of course, avoid pronouns altogether by writing something like "A says this, B says that; considering all the evidence, B's position seems more valid."

"I" is not the appropriate pronoun to use in a general statement that any informed reader would take for granted. Consider the following sentences.

> As I look at the number of cantatas Bach composed in his first few years at Leipzig, I am astounded.
>
> As we look at the number of cantatas . . . , we are astounded.
>
> As one looks at the number of cantatas . . . , one is astounded.

The first version, using "I," doesn't feel right; it sounds simultaneously arrogant and naive. The writer did not personally discover that Bach wrote an astounding number of cantatas in his first years at Leipzig; the chronology of Bach's cantatas is common knowledge and has been in print for years. Emphasizing your astonishment simply points out that you are new to the research game. Both "we" and "one" are adequate for sentences like this, but people object to both. "We" can sound pretentious, as if the writer were using the "royal we," as in "We are not amused." Some are uncomfortable with "one," feeling that it is stiff or old-fashioned, but I think it still works in general statements of this sort. If choosing a pronoun makes you uncomfortable, find another way to write the sentence—you can always find another way to say anything. In this case, you can avoid using any pronouns by turning the sentence around.

> The number of cantatas composed by Bach . . . is astounding.

In summary, use "I" when the idea is really yours, when you are sharing your own views, and when you are stating your conclusions, based on your research and analysis. Use other pronouns, or avoid pronouns altogether, when you are making more general statements. "The present writer" should be relegated to the dustbin with other phrases no longer in use.

Finally, there are two excellent ways to get a sense of the proper tone and level of sophistication in your writing. The first is to browse through journal articles with an eye for the tone of the writing; scholars present their ideas as clearly and forcefully as they can. The way to judge the tone of your own writing is to put the draft aside for a few days and reread it when you are somewhat removed from the act of drafting your ideas. After a pause of a few days, inappropriate language is generally quite clear. When you return to an old paper a week, a month, or a year later, the passages of slangy or pretentious language are obvious and embarrassing. Whenever you sit down to draft a paper, try to assume the frame of mind of a serious, competent scholar, trying to explain as clearly as possible important ideas about the art of music.

WRITING EFFECTIVE SENTENCES

The act of writing, whether the work is expository prose, fiction, or poetry, consists of choosing and assembling the words that will convey one's ideas as effectively as possible. In a way, the writer's responsibility boils down to choosing the next word, just as the composer's task ultimately consists of deciding what the next note or chord should be. Our discussion of writing style therefore begins at the level of choosing appropriate words and then moves on to combinations of words and questions of sentence structure.

Word Choice

The basic work of writing is the selection of appropriate words to convey the idea you have in mind. Care and precision in choosing the right words is what makes the difference between a convincing paper and one that is weak or dull. There are a few general principles that will help you make appropriate choices.

First, bear in mind that the English language, because of its long and involved history, is richer in vocabulary and synonyms than many other languages. Over the centuries, English has adopted words from Anglo-

Saxon, old Scandinavian languages, Norman French, Greek, Latin, modern French and German, Spanish, Italian, Arabic, and a host of other languages. You therefore have at your disposal an incredible wealth of synonyms for any word or idea, each with its own particular flavor and force. Browsing through a dictionary or a thesaurus gives one a sense of the vast vocabulary of English; most of us use only a tiny fraction of the words available to us. The huge vocabulary of modern English means that there is no reason to settle for awkward or inappropriate words, or words that do not quite fit the idea. Here are some specific recommendations about word choice.

Slang Use words in their original senses; avoid any slang usage that is different from a word's standard sense. Slang changes rapidly; as soon as the general population adopts a colorful slang usage, the group that originated it feels compelled to stop using it and invent new ways to keep their language private. In a formal paper, avoid using normal words in their slang senses, and, of course, avoid words that exist only in slang. "Twelve-tone music is so over!" may be fine in a conversation, and "over" is a legitimate English word, but this is a slang usage of the word and would not pass muster in a paper. Even the slang words that are acceptable in some contexts in the musical world, such as "fiddle" for "violin" and "chops" for "technical competence," should not be used in formal papers.

Anglo-Saxon and Latin roots Words derived from Anglo-Saxon roots are usually shorter, more concrete, and more forceful than words derived from Latin roots. "Church music" is more forceful than "ecclesiastical music"; "went mad" is stronger than "suffered a complete personality disintegration." I remember a counselor, worried about a troubled teenager, saying, "His emotional stability factors are in severe imbalance." I can think of crisper, livelier ways to put that, perhaps "That kid needs help" or "Watch out for that one." You cannot avoid Latin roots altogether, any more than you can avoid technical terms, but always stop to consider whether you can find a simpler, livelier way to say what you want to say.

Foreign words Foreign words may sometimes be unavoidable in your prose. Since many foreign words have no exact equivalent in English, using a foreign term may be the best way, or the only way, to say exactly what you want to say. It is a mistake, however, to use foreign words just for effect. A flood of foreign words gives your prose a stuffy and pedantic flavor and creates the impression that you are more interested in showing off your erudition than in communicating your ideas. Consider the following sentence.

> The *Weltschmerz* that permeates the early songs is in keeping with the *Zeitgeist* of *fin-de-siècle* Vienna.

That sentence tells us more about the author's pretensions to learning than about Vienna or the songs in question. Although you can convey the same idea using standard English words, you might choose to retain one of the foreign terms, since their meanings are different in subtle ways from the standard English translations, and some foreign words almost defy translation. In revising this sentence, you might decide to keep either *Weltschmerz* or *fin-de-siècle* because of its particular nuance or connotation. An occasional foreign word is fine; a string of them is pretentious.

Use words literally   Respect the literal force of words. "Unique," for example, means "the only one in the world." Therefore, to describe a movement or a musical phenomenon as "somewhat unique" or "totally unique" is meaningless; it is impossible to be somewhat unique, just as it is impossible to be somewhat dead. "Hopefully" means "in a spirit of hope," not "I hope that." Thus a sentence like "Hopefully, the performance will reach a higher level once the orchestra has a few more rehearsals" makes no sense. "Decimate" is widely used as a synonym for "devastate," in sentences like "The town was decimated by the flood." "Decimate," from the Latin *decimus* ("tenth"), means to destroy ten percent of something; it describes, for example, the practice used by occupying armies to punish resistance by lining up the inhabitants of a town and arbitrarily killing every tenth person. Since I first drafted this section, the battles over "hopefully" and "decimate" may have been lost; careless usage may once again have forced a change in the rules. I still think a careful writer should use words correctly, whether the world at large does or not. We could go on with other examples, but the point is clear—respect the literal meaning of the words you use.

Creating new words   Use existing words; there is no reason to create new words by piling prefixes or suffixes onto existing words. In everyday English, there is a tendency to tack "-ize" or "-wise" onto every other word. The resulting neologisms, such as "prioritize," "finalize," and "background-wise," are ugly and unnecessary. The writer should be able to find a respectable English word or phrase that will convey that same idea in a more natural and graceful manner. Sometimes music students create awkward hybrids such as "analyzation," "texture-wise," and "a minuet-type movement." "Analyzation" is not even a real word; I suspect it is an attempt to create a Latinate form of the term "analysis," which is a borrowed Greek word. Actually, if you want to sound educated and profound, Greek trumps Latin every time, so "analysis" is perfect as it is. "Texture-wise" and "minuet-type" are clumsy and unnecessary. Take the trouble to find the appropriate word from the rich vocabulary of standard English, and do not resort to artificial and ungainly creations.

In musicological studies based on new critical methodologies, one sees strange new words constructed by adding suffixes to familiar roots—words such as "narrativity," "narratology," "commodification," "contextualization," and even "recontextualization." These words, however, are not careless substitutes for ordinary English words; they were created because the new critical approaches needed a new technical vocabulary. That process is different from jamming roots and suffixes together to create your own new words for no reason.

Nouns are nouns and verbs are verbs Respecting what words mean includes using words as their proper parts of speech. There is a tendency in some areas of modern English to make nouns out of verbs, verbs out of nouns, adjectives out of nouns or verbs, and so forth. "All systems are definitely in a go configuration" may be normal language at NASA headquarters, but it is unacceptable in a paper; "go" is a verb, not an adjective. "He's their go-to guy" appears regularly in sports pages, but "go-to" is a very odd adjective, not something you would use in a paper. Similarly, "That was a fun rehearsal" may be fine in conversation, but you can't say, *"The Barber of Seville* is a fun opera" in a paper, since "fun" is a noun, not an adjective. In standard English, "access" is a noun, not a verb; "I was unable to access the primary sources" is standard language in computer science classes, but not in a humanities paper. That last example, turning a noun into a verb, represents a common recent tendency. One reads, for example, that music "transitions" from one section to another and groups meet to "interface," "dialogue," and "conference" with each other. In the new schools of critical theory, scholars "gender" texts and write that Eurocentric literature courses "privilege" the works of white male writers. I assume that the justification for this practice is that these artificial verbs are needed as new technical terms. All the words in quotation marks in those sentences are nouns hijacked into service as verbs, a practice some call "verbing." The perfect comment on verbing appeared in a now-defunct comic strip called *Calvin and Hobbes,* when one character announced, "Verbing weirds language." Use nouns as nouns and verbs as verbs.

Word Combinations

Variety of word choice It is not enough to choose the right individual word; sometimes a perfectly appropriate word is inappropriate in context because it already appears in the previous phrase or is used nearby in another sense. Consider the following sentence.

> Works by twenty-five composers appear in the collection of works our seminar is working on, and the fact that there are no weak works speaks highly of the work of these composers.

That sentence sounds strange and ungainly because of the repetition of the same word. It can easily be repaired by using synonyms.

> Works by twenty-five composers appear in the collection the seminar is studying, and the fact that there are no weak pieces speaks highly of the skill of these composers.

This issue is complicated further when one writes about music; one must reserve the words used as technical musical terms for that use alone, and not try to use them as ordinary English words. You will confuse your reader if you use *key, major, minor, development,* and other technical terms both as general English words and as special musical terms. Sentences like the following cause confusion.

> The key element in sonata-allegro structure is the element of key.
>
> One of the new developments in the Romantic symphony is the emphasis on the development sections.

Those sentences can easily be rewritten, using the musical terms only in their technical senses and substituting synonyms when those words are used in a nonmusical sense.

> The determining factor in sonata-allegro structure is the element of key.
>
> One important change in the Romantic symphony is the new emphasis on development sections.

Noun strings   There is a tendency in modern English to create phrases out of strings of loosely related nouns. We have already mentioned "revenue enhancement strategies" and "curriculum evaluation criteria," which are at the same time awkward noun strings and inflated, pretentious phrases. The Department of Agriculture, concerned about the presence in schools of vending machines filled with chips and snack cakes, referred to these foods as "low-nutrition density options" instead of the standard two-syllable term, "junk food." In papers on music, one sees phrases like "the composer control issue," "remote key area harmonies," and "the patron/composer relationship." A slash or a hyphen between two juxtaposed nouns does not solve the problem; those phrases are still strings of vaguely related nouns, not correct English phrases. To make standard English of a noun string, rearrange the words, using prepositional phrases, apostrophes, or other grammatical means to express the relationship between the different nouns. The preceding examples can be rewritten as "the issue of the composer's control," "chords in remote keys," "the relationship between patron and composer," or other logical alternatives.

Redundant couplets   In modern English one frequently sees adjective-and-noun combinations in which the two words mean the same thing. Common examples are "general consensus," "subject matter," and "end result." In each case, one of the words is unnecessary padding. Consensus, for example, is by definition general—there can be no such thing as a private consensus; the same logic applies to the other examples. Avoid these padded constructions. Papers on music often use a peculiar couplet—"in-depth analysis," which is objectionable for two reasons. First, *in-depth* is a stale catch phrase; it is also an artificial adjective constructed by jamming together a preposition and its object. Second, the phrase is redundant; all analysis is necessarily "in-depth," since analysis means breaking a phenomenon down into its parts and studying each in detail. Also avoid redundant prefixes in creations such as "interrelationship." "Inter-," a prefix borrowed from Latin, means "between"; since relationships exist only between two or more entities, the prefix is unnecessary.

Stock couplets   Stock couplets are combinations of adjectives and nouns that always seem to appear together. "Abject poverty," "utter despair," "reckless abandon," and "extenuating circumstances" are common examples. By now, "extenuating" seems to have lost its meaning of "helping to explain or excuse" and has become a meaningless appendage routinely attached to the word "circumstances." One student's concert report contained the following sentence.

> Unfortunately the first piece listed on the program was not performed because of extenuating circumstances.

I assume that the student meant "unforeseen" or "unavoidable" circumstances. Try to avoid stock couplets because of the flabbiness of these overused phrases. When describing music, find alternatives for such stock phrases as "lyrical second theme" and "dramatic opening gesture."

The "not un-" construction   Avoid the "not un-" construction, as in "It was not uncommon during the Renaissance for composers to begin their careers as choirboys in the chapels of the great courts." That construction is weak and affected, and overuse of it rapidly becomes, in the famous words of Strunk and White, "not unannoying."

Dependence on modifiers   In general, rely on strong nouns and verbs rather than modifiers to convey your ideas. One sure way to tighten up your writing is to eliminate all qualifying adverbs, such as *somewhat, virtually, literally, perhaps,* and *very.* If the nouns and verbs have been chosen with care, qualifiers rarely add anything to the sentence; in fact, they weaken the force of your writing. If you choose strong, colorful verbs, you won't have to rely on modifiers. Consider the following sentences.

> The conductor walked quickly to the podium, raised his arms, and briskly led the orchestra in the loud, dramatic opening of the tone poem.

> The conductor bounded to the podium, raised his arms, and unleashed the full fury of the orchestra.

The second sentence, whatever else you might think of it, is certainly tighter and livelier than the first, because it relies on strong verbs—"bounded" and "unleashed"—to paint the desired picture. I mentioned earlier that English is a language rich in synonyms; if you stop and think for a minute, you can find many colorful synonyms for a word like "walk." Let me suggest a few alternatives; try to create more yourself. The conductor "marched" to the podium, or "leapt," "pranced," "strode," "lurched," "plodded," "swiveled" through the violins, "raced," "danced," "shuffled," "charged."

Lately, spoken English seems to rely not only on single modifiers but also on loosely connected modifying phrases, introduced by words such as "in terms of" or "as to," to bear the weight of the sentence. One hears and reads sentences like the following.

> The new principal horn will be a great addition to the orchestra, in terms of her mastery of technique and her beautiful tone.
>
> The new conductor is doing wonderful work from the standpoint of precision and the ensemble sound.

Those sentences are weak; in both cases, the real point comes only at the end, after a loose connective that serves as useless filler. If you see weak sentences like this in your own writing, stop for a moment, think about what you are really trying to say, and then make the important ideas the subject or the verb of the sentence, not a loosely attached afterthought. Here are some revised versions; there are other ways to make stronger sentences out of these two examples.

> Her rock-solid technique and beautiful tone make the new principal horn a great addition to the orchestra.
>
> The new principal horn, with her technical mastery and beautiful tone, will be a great addition to the orchestra.
>
> The new conductor has greatly improved the orchestra's precision and ensemble sound.
>
> The orchestra's new precision and ensemble sound are a tribute to the new conductor's ability.

One reason we rely so much on modifiers to convey our ideas is that many of the words we use constantly have lost their force. "A brilliant performance" sounds like high praise, but if you describe as "brilliant" any performance in which the players manage to end more or less together, then you have to find something stronger, like "exceptionally brilliant," to describe a truly superior performance. If everyone who has ever set foot on a stage, appeared in a film, or made a recording is called a "star," then exceptional performers have to be classified as "superstars." Once "superstar" has been cheapened by being applied to everyone in the business, we will need still another category—perhaps "megastar" or "demigod." If you choose strong, colorful nouns and verbs, you can eliminate useless modifiers, you will need fewer words to convey your ideas, and your writing will become tighter, more forceful, and more effective.

Sentence Structure

Writing effective expository prose is not simply a matter of choosing the right words. No matter how appropriate each word is, your prose may still be boring or difficult to understand, depending on how you deal with the matter of sentence structure.

Passive voice   One kind of sentence structure that frequently weakens student prose is the passive voice. Some students seem to feel that constructions based on the passive voice are especially appropriate, or even required, in scholarly writing. The passive voice is not always wrong; it is the correct choice when you want to emphasize the action itself, rather than the subject who is performing the action. Compare the following sentences.

American opera companies frequently perform *Peter Grimes.*

Britten's *Peter Grimes* is performed regularly by American opera companies.

If your point is that *Peter Grimes,* in contrast to most twentieth-century operas, has become part of the standard repertoire, the second sentence, passive voice and all, is a clearer way to state your idea. The first version is not exactly the same and seems to emphasize the idea that American opera companies perform the work, as opposed to English or German companies.

Some uses of passive voice, like the following impersonal constructions, are especially weak.

It has often been stated . . .

In this study, several examples of the Baroque concerto grosso have been analyzed.

John Cage has frequently been viewed as . . .

Each of the preceding sentences is vague and awkward. The reader naturally wonders who is responsible for the various actions: Who has often stated this, viewed Cage in this way, or analyzed these concerti grossi?

Passive voice is not always wrong, but you should have a good reason for using it. Generally, the active voice, with a clear subject, verb, and object, is more forceful and direct. Avoid those impersonal "it" constructions altogether.

Word order   Since English grammar depends on word order rather than on inflected endings to indicate the case of nouns, changing the word order changes the meaning you convey, in both gross and subtle ways. Consider the different force and emphasis of the following sentences.

1. After the large-scale works of his early period, Stravinsky turned to a new idiom, the neoclassical style, which represents his chief contribution to twentieth-century music.
2. After the large-scale works of his early period, which represent his chief contribution to twentieth-century music, Stravinsky turned to a new idiom, the neoclassical style.
3. Stravinsky turned to a new idiom, the neoclassical style, which represents his chief contribution to twentieth-century music, after the large-scale works of his early period.
4. After the large-scale works of his early period, Stravinsky turned to a new idiom, his chief contribution to twentieth-century style—neoclassicism.

The first sentence is perfectly clear, and the word order is acceptable. The second version, by putting the subordinate clause after "period" rather than "idiom," changes the idea entirely; now the sentence states that the large-scale early works, rather than the neoclassical works, represent Stravinsky's chief contribution to twentieth-century music. The third version is correct but weak, since, after making its point, the sentence trails off with a relatively unimportant adverbial phrase. The fourth version is the strongest, since it puts the important term, "neoclassicism," in the strong final position. When you edit your work, try changing the order of elements in your sentences until the words not only say what you want to say but also say it with the exact shade of emphasis that you intend. Word order is related to correct placement of modifiers, whether they are single words, phrases, or clauses; I will deal with that topic in the next chapter.

Parallel constructions   When you want to emphasize the relationship between parallel elements or ideas, or the contrast between them, keep the sentence structure parallel. Consider the following sentence.

> Typical examples of the symphonic poem are *Les Préludes* by Liszt and *Ein Heldenleben* by Strauss; another example is Smetana's *Má Vlast*.

The problem with that sentence is that Smetana seems to be added as an afterthought or placed in a secondary, subsidiary position. The reader wonders exactly what the writer meant to say. The idea is much clearer when the series is kept in parallel construction.

> Typical examples of the symphonic poem are *Les Préludes* by Liszt, *Ein Heldenleben* by Strauss, and *Má Vlast* by Smetana.

Parallel construction is also the clearest way to emphasize the contrast between two ideas. Compare the following sentences.

> Bach, a church musician, composed cantatas and Passions; Handel, on the other hand, did not specialize in those genres, but rather in opera and oratorio. The explanation for this difference is that Handel worked for the English court rather than the church.

> Bach, a church musician, composed cantatas and Passions; Handel, a court musician, composed operas and oratorios.

The second sentence, with its tight parallel structure, states the contrast between the two composers much more clearly and strongly than the first sentence.

When you are trying to utilize parallel construction, you must also be sure that all the elements match grammatically. If the first element consists of a verb and its object, then each of the later elements must be constructed the same way. You cannot put different grammatical units in parallel. The parallel elements need not be the same length, but all the elements must be grammatically parallel. Consider the following sentences.

> **Wrong:** His favorite pastimes are listening to music, chess, and to go on hikes.

> **Correct:** His favorite pastimes are listening to music, playing chess, and hiking.

Correct: His favorite pastimes are music, chess, and the outdoors.

Correct: His favorite pastimes are listening to music, especially Baroque music and jazz, playing chess, and hiking.

Parallel constructions can be very effective, particularly when you are trying to make an important point in your argument. It takes some time and care to set up parallel constructions correctly, but it is well worth the effort if the effect is strong and persuasive.

Variety of sentence structure Just as well-chosen words will not produce effective prose if sentence structure is not handled correctly, individually correct sentences will not result in effective paragraphs unless there is variety in the sentence structure. A series of short, subject-verb-object sentences is, at best, boring; a string of long, involved sentences makes it unduly difficult for the reader to follow your thought. Since any structure becomes tiresome when it turns into an invariable pattern, one key to effective writing is to vary the sentence structure. Consider the following paragraphs.

> William Byrd was born in Lincolnshire in 1543. He studied with Thomas Tallis. He was appointed organist of Lincoln Cathedral in 1568. He was elected a member of the Chapel Royal in 1570.

> William Byrd was born, probably in Lincolnshire, although the documentary proof of this fact is less than definitive, in 1543. It is commonly assumed, in the absence of incontrovertible proof, that he studied music with Thomas Tallis, another organist, Gentleman of the Chapel Royal under several English monarchs, and co-holder with Byrd of a royal patent for the publication of music, although that of course did not occur until much later, after Byrd had begun his career as an organist and been himself elected to the post of Gentleman of the Chapel Royal, while still retaining his organ position, at least for some years.

The first paragraph is choppy and childish. The second is needlessly complex and unfocused. By the time readers finish that second rambling sentence, with all its afterthoughts, qualifiers, and digressions, they no longer know or care who the original subject was. When your syntax gets that tangled, stop, back up, and think about exactly what you want to say. Much of that material should be eliminated, and the syntax should be greatly simplified.

Complex sentences divide statements into main ideas and subordinate or secondary clauses. Since complex sentences single out one action as the main idea, they are generally clearer and stronger than compound sentences, which treat all the ideas as equal in importance. Compare the following sentences.

> Byrd studied music with Thomas Tallis, then he was appointed organist of Lincoln Cathedral, and shortly thereafter he was elected a Gentleman of the Chapel Royal.

> After he studied music with Thomas Tallis and served as organist of Lincoln Cathedral, Byrd was elected a Gentleman of the Chapel Royal in 1570.

The first sentence treats the three events as a series of equally important ideas, and the effect is choppy. The second pushes the material about Byrd's training and early career into the background in a subordinate clause and puts the main emphasis on Byrd's appointment to the Chapel Royal. What the sentence really wants to say should be the main clause; put the rest into subordinate clauses or modifying phrases.

You can see why the process of writing and editing takes time. The struggle to find exactly the right word and exactly the right grammatical structure to convey what you want to say, and with the proper emphasis, takes time and effort. Once you have a series of good sentences, you also must worry about variety of sentence structure. Whenever the structure of a sentence is confusing, back away for a moment and focus on exactly what you are trying to say. Once your ideas are clear, you should be able to find language that will convey them clearly and effectively.

EFFECTIVE PARAGRAPHS

A paragraph is more than a series of correct sentences; it is a unified exposition or explanation of a single idea. A paragraph focuses on a single thought, and its chief quality must be coherence. The paragraph must have a topic sentence that clearly states the single idea the paragraph will develop, and the rest of the paragraph must be closely related to that single idea. When you are editing your prose, check the paragraphs for unity; if there is anything in a paragraph that does not relate closely to the topic sentence, delete the unrelated material or find another place for it. If a paragraph begins by discussing one idea and then moves into an extended discussion of a second idea, make that discussion of the second idea a new paragraph with its own topic sentence. Read through the following paragraph.

> Mahler's Second Symphony, also known as the "Resurrection" Symphony, is one of his best-known works. Following the example of Beethoven's Ninth Symphony, Mahler uses voices in the final climactic section of the work. After a long, agitated, and highly developed first movement, there follows an Andante in the easy, folksonglike rhythm of an Austrian *Ländler.* The third movement is a symphonic adaptation of one of the *Wunderhorn* songs, and the brief fourth movement is a new setting, for contralto solo, of still another poem from this collection. The finale, after a vivid orchestral section depicting the day of Resurrection, leads to a monumental setting for soloists and chorus of a Resurrection ode by the eighteenth-century German poet Klopstock. This finale is reminiscent of Part II of the Eighth Symphony, a monumental movement for soloists and chorus, which nearly constitutes a complete secular oratorio. As other examples of secular oratorios, one might cite the "Faust" Symphony by Liszt, usually classified as a program symphony; his oratorio *St. Elizabeth,* which perhaps is difficult to fit into the "secular" classification; and even Wagner's *Parsifal.*

The errors in this paragraph should be obvious. Earlier in this chapter, I discussed ungainly expressions like "folksonglike"; here our concern is coherence. After a brief description of each of the movements of the Second Symphony, the author suddenly wanders off into a discussion of Part II of the Eighth Symphony. The similarity of the Second and Eighth symphonies certainly deserves brief mention, like the earlier reference to Beethoven, but the last two sentences go far beyond brief mention. By introducing the provocative notion that the secular oratorio is an important genre and then arguing that this genre includes such works as a program symphony, a religious oratorio, and an opera, the writer has let the digression go much too far. The last sentence is filled with complex ideas that have little to do with Mahler's Second Symphony and call for much more explanation and justification than the writer provides. The reader is distracted and confused by this material. Those last sentences should be shortened considerably, and perhaps the writer should consider eliminating the discussion of the finale of the Eighth Symphony. If that comparison is useful to the topic and demands some explanation, it should be discussed in a separate paragraph. One of the major tasks of the editing process is cutting and pasting—moving sentences and ideas from one paragraph to another or from one section to another, so that each paragraph is a logical unit and all the material relevant to each point is grouped in one place.

THE EFFECTIVE ESSAY

Earlier, in Chapter 4, in the section on outlining a paper, we looked at the elements that make a good essay; that same material merits brief mention here to complete our discussion of the qualities of a good essay.

A series of paragraphs related to a single topic does not of itself constitute a good essay. The paragraphs must be ordered and connected in such a way that the argument moves along logically. The order in which ideas are presented makes a difference in the effectiveness of the essay as a whole. Like each paragraph, the entire essay must have a thesis, expressed in the central topic sentence; that thesis will determine which paragraphs should be included and which should be cut, as well as suggesting the order in which the material should be discussed.

In the process of turning a series of paragraphs into an essay, the writer needs to add some material to create the large-scale unity the essay must have.

Introduction

An essay cannot begin with the first paragraph of the main body of discussion. The essay needs an introduction that will lead into the topic, state the main thesis of the essay, and outline for the reader how the essay will proceed and what kinds of argumentation will be used. Introductions often begin with a general statement, move to the particular area the essay will discuss, and then state the thesis that the essay will defend. Introductions can also move in the opposite direction, from mention of a particular detail to discussion of a more general idea, followed by the thesis of the essay.

A good introduction avoids two extremes. It is wrong to start abruptly, so that the reader has no chance to see what you plan to do and where your topic fits in the larger view of the history of music. It is also wrong to get so carried away with your introductory ideas that the introduction becomes a long, independent essay or brings up ideas and arguments that will not be taken up later in the essay. It is difficult to generalize about the proper length for an introduction; style guides generally state that the introduction should be about one-tenth of the complete essay. Sometimes, of course, a longer introduction may be necessary to clarify complex concepts or terms that are essential to your argument.

Transitions

The reader of an essay should know at all times where he or she is in the course of the argument and where this particular material fits into the overall discussion. Therefore, it is usually necessary to add transitional material as you move from one subordinate topic to another. The reader has to know when the introduction is over and the main body of the paper is beginning; the reader also must be aware that you are moving from one argument to another in the body of the paper. Transitions need not be elaborate or long; a word or two, a phrase, or a clause may be enough to indicate a shift of ideas. Simply leaping from one argument to another is awkward and confusing. Paragraphs and ideas are not connected into a unified argument by simple proximity; they need to be joined together gracefully. The relationship between sections and the reader's position in the logical chain of argumentation must be clear at all times.

Conclusion

An essay of any length must be summarized in a concluding section. If the essay trails off with the last paragraph of argumentation, readers are left with a feeling of incompleteness and, left on their own, must somehow gather all the detailed exposition and argumentation into a single, coherent whole. The conclusion need not be as long as the introduction and need not be world-shaking. Some sort of closing section, however, is necessary.

To understand the necessity for a concluding section, consider the analogy with musical structure. The longer a composer has sustained tension and suspense in a piece, the longer the final resolution needs to be. The short and matter-of-fact codas appended to classical symphonic movements would never suffice to conclude the longer and more dramatic movements of the Romantic period. In the latter, since so much accumulated tension has been built up, the listener needs a proportionally longer period of resolution and calm. When you move from short paragraphs to an essay of ten or twenty or thirty pages, the reader needs a proportionally longer introduction and conclusion to tie all the ideas together into a convincing statement.

One final warning about writing style in concluding sections. The conclusion should be written in the same tone and style as the rest of the essay. Since conclusions are difficult to write, students sometimes resort to a hortatory or flowery tone that is inconsistent with the tone and style of the rest of the essay. Remember that the purpose of expository prose is to inform and explain, not to preach, urge the audience to action, or dramatize. Maintain the same competent, informed, and professional tone as the rest of the essay, and bring your work to a clear and forceful close.

SUMMARY

Each level of writing—the individual word, the sentence, the paragraph, and the essay—has its own stylistic demands and requires the writer's careful attention. At every stage of producing a paper, including planning, drafting, and editing, the writer must be attentive to the specific demands of that level. Variety of sentence structure, coherence and unity in the paragraphs, and a clear overall organization, with a helpful introduction, transitions, and conclusion, are just as important as the choice of individual words. Carelessness at any of these levels can defeat the purpose of your work and the care and precision exercised at the other levels. An effective prose style results from the writer's understanding of the challenges present at each of these levels and success at meeting those challenges. Read articles in the standard journals with an eye to large-scale organization; note how the author introduces the subject and the thesis, and see how transitions and the conclusion link all the paragraphs into a single argument. Once again, be aware that good writing is a complex process, requiring work at several different levels and several separate stages.

CHAPTER 8

Common Writing Problems

This chapter discusses problems that are common in student papers—both general writing problems and the special problems that trouble students writing about music. Although these issues may seem elementary to some readers, they occur frequently in papers at both the undergraduate and the graduate levels. I have included only a selection of such problems, drawn from my experience reading student prose. The standard guides to writing style, such as *The Chicago Manual of Style* and the *Simon & Schuster Handbook for Writers*, contain much more detailed advice on writing correctly and precisely. We will deal first with basic writing errors, and then with the special problems connected with writing about music.

ERRORS IN BASIC GRAMMAR AND WRITING

Incomplete Sentences

To constitute a complete sentence, a group of words must have at least a subject and a predicate. Some student papers contain incomplete sentences like the following.

> Byrd, after studying with Thomas Tallis, a Gentleman of the Chapel Royal, being appointed a cathedral organist, and later winning a position as a court composer.

> Impressionism can be understood as an extension of the late Romantic aesthetic expressed through new musical means. Likewise with expressionism.

These examples represent the two situations in which incomplete sentences or sentence fragments usually occur. The first consists of the subject followed by a long subordinate clause or a string of participial phrases. The writer forgets that he or she has left the subject hanging there without a main verb. The second example starts with a perfectly good sentence but then adds a shorthand afterthought as a separate unit. This sort of construction is common in spoken style, but it will not pass muster in a formal paper. The second idea must be rewritten as a complete sentence.

Run-on Sentences

The opposite error is to jam too many subjects and verbs into the same sentence, without the proper punctuation or conjunction necessary to separate the complete sentences or clauses.

> Ockeghem wrote extremely long lines, with widely spaced cadences, Josquin constructed lines that have a much clearer phrase structure and regularly occurring cadences.

What is written as one long sentence is actually two complete sentences, and the comma is not sufficient punctuation to separate them. This sort of construction often appears with an adverb such as "however" or "yet" in the second half, after the comma. Even with the adverb, that is still a run-on sentence. It is relatively easy to correct this mistake; following are several correct ways to state the same idea.

> Whereas Ockeghem usually wrote extremely long lines with widely spaced cadences, Josquin composed lines . . .
>
> Ockeghem usually wrote extremely long lines . . . ; Josquin, however, composed lines . . .
>
> Ockeghem usually wrote . . . no clear phrase structure. Josquin, on the other hand, composed lines that have . . .

Note that it is always possible to break a run-on sentence into two sentences. If you want to keep the two clauses in the same sentence, you have two choices. You can form a compound sentence by connecting the two main clauses with either a conjunction or a semicolon, or you can form a complex sentence by turning one into a subordinate clause and keeping the other as the main clause. In a complex sentence, a comma is sufficient punctuation between the two clauses.

Agreement: Subject and Verb

One of the fundamental rules in most languages is that the subject and the verb must agree in number. Students sometimes break this basic rule, usually in long and unwieldy constructions that blur the identity of the real subject. Consider the following sentence.

> No innovative composer, not even the twentieth-century composers usually classified as members of the avant-garde, such as Cage, Stockhausen, and Wuorinen, have ever totally abandoned their musical roots.

Here the singular subject ("No composer") is buried under the subsequent verbiage, with its plural nouns and the series of names; by the time the writer finally gets to the verb, he or she is thinking in the plural. If you correct the sentence by using a singular verb ("has ever totally abandoned"), the sentence is correct but sounds awkward and ungainly. In such a situation, cross out the whole thing and start again, first forming a clearer idea of exactly what you want to say.

If the subject is a collective noun, such as "committee," "quartet," or "orchestra," choosing the proper number for the verb is not always a straightforward question. As a general rule, collective nouns take singular verbs when the group is thought of as a unit acting together.

> This orchestra has a real flair for late Romantic music.
>
> The committee recommends that Professor Smith be awarded tenure.

When the group is thought of as a collection of individuals acting separately, the collective noun takes a plural verb. The following sentences sound strange but are actually correct, because the members of the group are acting as separate individuals.

> Once the orchestra pack up their instruments and go home, they seem to forget everything they learned in the rehearsal.
>
> Since the committee fight constantly over every tiny question, they rarely accomplish anything.

The easiest way to smooth out these awkward-sounding sentences is to add a plural noun, such as "members"; thus:

> Once the orchestra players pack up their instruments and go home, they seem to forget everything they learned in the rehearsal.
>
> Since the members of the committee fight constantly over every small question, they rarely accomplish anything.

Agreement: Pronoun and Antecedent

Pronouns must agree with their antecedents in number. That straightforward rule usually is easy enough to follow, but two special situations often cause problems for writers.

In the first situation, the writer must choose the proper pronoun for collective nouns like the examples in the previous section. Collective nouns considered as a single group take singular pronouns; when thought of as a collection of individuals, they take plural pronouns. In the first two sentences below, the groups designated by the collective nouns are thought of as acting as units; since the antecedents are singular, the pronouns referring to them are singular as well. The antecedents in sentences 3 and 4 are also collective nouns, but the groups are treated as individuals acting separately; the possessive pronouns referring to them are therefore plural. Once again, addition of a plural noun helps.

1. The orchestra has worked very hard to refine its sound.
2. The Executive Committee insists on its right to review all decisions affecting departmental policy.
3. The quartet (players) spend too much time tuning their instruments between movements, breaking the flow of the music.
4. The committee (members) cannot agree on how to discharge their responsibilities.

In the second situation, the writer must choose one pronoun to refer to both genders.

Every student must bring his anthology to each class meeting.

Any student wishing to enter the concerto competition must submit his application by October 15.

The use of a masculine pronoun to refer to any human being, masculine or feminine, used to be acceptable, but then orchestras consisting only of old white men, with perhaps a woman or two playing the harp or the flute, seemed natural to us too. In today's world of equality, we need gender-neutral language that will not treat "composer," "conductor," "performer," "department chair," "dean," and similar words as masculine nouns. In the same way, we need to find a way to write general statements that is not gender-biased. Some people have proposed using a gender-neutral plural pronoun, even with the singular antecedent, thus:

Any student wishing to enter the concerto competition must submit their application by October 15.

That solution is incorrect and unnecessary; there are several ways to avoid biased language besides abandoning all logic and the rules of syntax. This sentence can easily be rewritten in a way that avoids both gender bias and incorrect grammar. Actually, this particular sentence can be rewritten without any pronoun, avoiding the problem altogether.

Any student wishing to enter the concerto competition must submit an application by October 15.

When that strategy is not available and the sentence doesn't work without a pronoun, there are several standard ways to avoid the masculine pronoun.

1. Make the sentence plural.

Students wishing to enter the concerto competition must submit their applications by October 15.

2. Put the sentence in the second person.

If you wish to enter the concerto competition, you must submit an application by October 15.

3. Put the sentence in the passive voice, if possible.

   Applications from those wishing to enter the concerto competition must be submitted by October 15.

4. Rewrite the sentence so that no pronouns are necessary.

   The deadline for applications for the concerto competition is October 15.

Proper Cases of Pronouns

English, unlike some other languages, does not use cases for its nouns; it does, however, retain case-specific forms for some pronouns. These pronouns have three cases—nominative, possessive, and objective; the writer chooses the correct form based on the grammatical function of the pronoun in its context. The case-specific forms that we still use are listed in the following table.

Nominative	Possessive	Objective
I	my	me
he	his	him
she	her	her
they	their	them
who	whose	whom
whoever	whosever	whomever

Some writers seem to choose from among these forms by instinct or sound rather than by the grammatical function of the pronoun in the sentence. One hears incorrect cases frequently in compound phrases like the following.

   My parents frequently took my brother and I to concerts and plays.

   The conductor offered George and I the opportunity to join the trombone section for the next concert.

In the first sentence, "I" is the direct object of the verb "took"; in the second, "I" is the indirect object of the verb "offered." In both cases, therefore, the nominative case is wrong; it should be the objective form—"me." People who would never say "They took I to concerts" or "He offered I" somehow feel that "I" always sounds more educated in compound phrases like these, whatever case is required by the context. If you have trouble deciding the correct form in sentences like this, separate the compound phrase into its components or review the simple rules about the proper cases of pronouns.

Relative Pronouns

The grammar books define relative pronouns as pronouns that introduce adjectival clauses and some kinds of noun clauses; among the important relative pronouns are "who," "which," "that," "what," and "whoever."

"Who," "which," and "that" are used to introduce adjectival clauses that tell us more about an antecedent. "Who" is the correct relative pronoun when the antecedent is a person. "Which" and "that" usually refer to things or sometimes to groups of people when they are considered a collective unit. "Which" is usually used in nonrestrictive clauses—that is, in clauses that add information about the antecedent rather than specifying a general antecedent. "That" is usually used in restrictive clauses, those that make a general subject more specific. Restrictive clauses are not set off by commas; nonrestrictive clauses are. Therefore, "that" is usually correct in clauses without commas, and "which" is correct in clauses with commas. The following sentences illustrate the proper punctuation and choice of relative pronouns for the two types of clauses.

> *Otello,* which was one of Verdi's last operas, is written in a style considerably different from that of his earlier operas. [The clause is nonrestrictive; it simply adds more information.]
>
> The opera that made Verdi a success was *Nabucco.* [The clause is restrictive; it limits and specifies "opera," a general noun.]

The distinction between restrictive and nonrestrictive phrases and clauses is discussed in more detail later in this chapter, in the section on the correct use of the comma. For now, it is enough to connect "which" with nonrestrictive clauses and "that" with restrictive clauses.

In the table on page 126, note that "who" and "whoever" have case-specific forms. The choice of the correct form is based on the grammatical function of the pronoun in the context of the sentence. The following sentences are correct.

> Ockeghem, who taught many of the younger composers of his time . . .
>
> The patron in whose service he worked . . .
>
> The master whom he chose to imitate . . .
>
> The Grammy is usually awarded to whoever sold the most recordings that year.
>
> I will work with whomever the committee selects to fill the conducting position next year.

In the first sentence, "who" is the subject of "taught" and therefore is in the nominative case. In the second, "whose" is possessive, modifying "service." In the third sentence, "whom" is the object of the verb "chose," and therefore is in the objective case. In the fourth sentence, it might appear that "whoever" is the object of the preposition "to," and therefore should be in the objective case, but the entire noun clause that follows "to" is the object of the preposition. Within that clause, "whoever" is the subject of the verb "sold," and therefore is in the nominative case. In the fifth sentence, the noun clause beginning with "whomever" is the object of the preposition "with"; "whomever" is the object of the verb "selects" and therefore is in the objective case.

Sometimes the grammatical context is complicated by additional clauses. Consider the following sentences.

Whom do you think they will choose for the principal flute position?

The Dean is the one who we believe should have the final word on personnel issues.

In the first sentence, "whom" is correct because it is the direct object of the verb "will choose." In the second, "who" is the subject of "should have," and therefore is in the nominative case. The way to make these choices is to strip the sentence down to its basic elements—subject, verb, and object—and choose the correct form to fit the grammatical structure.

"Whom" is rarely used in casual conversation; in writing, one should still choose the proper case based on the grammatical context. Note the following sentences; most people would use the second version in conversation, but the first version is the correct one for written style.

She is a sensitive accompanist on whom you can always rely.

NOT

She is a sensitive accompanist who you can always rely on.

Misplaced Modifiers

Modifiers, whether they are single words, phrases, or clauses, can add important elements and color to your writing, but you must use care in locating them so that they are clearly connected with the appropriate words and ideas. Putting modifiers in the wrong place in the sentence can make nonsense or unintended comedy out of your sentences, and unfortunately is a frequent error in student prose.

Single words   "Only" is a useful and important adverb; for the sake of logic and clarity, it should be placed as close as possible to the word or idea that it modifies. In the following sentences, note how changing the location of "only" changes the meaning and emphasis of the sentence.

Only I attended the rehearsal yesterday. [No one else did.]

I only attended the rehearsal yesterday. [I didn't take part in it, record it, or do anything but watch.]

I attended only the rehearsal yesterday. [Not the performance.]

I attended the rehearsal only yesterday. [That recently.]

The common error in the use of "only" is to place it too early in the sentence, usually before the verb, when it actually belongs with a later word or phrase. "I only have eyes for you," the refrain of an old standard popular tune, illustrates this error; the sentence should read, "I have eyes only for you." Consider the following sentences.

Wrong: He only achieved success as a performer late in his life.

Correct: He achieved success as a performer only late in his life.

Misplaced phrases   A modifying phrase put in the wrong place can easily create an illogical or comic effect. Consider the following sentences.

Fortunately, my roommate found my wallet walking through the parking lot.

Lying in plain view right next to my car, my roommate found my wallet.

Both these sentences paint bizarre pictures. The first sentence has a wallet walking; the second has the roommate lying on the ground next to the car. "Walking" and "lying" are participles, which function both as verbs and as adjectives modifying nouns. They must be located near the nouns they modify. These strange sentences can easily be corrected by moving the modifying phrases to their proper places.

Fortunately, my roommate, walking through the parking lot, found my wallet.

My roommate found my wallet lying in plain view right next to my car.

One can also fix these sentences by changing the construction; one way is to turn the participial phrase into a clause with its own subject.

Fortunately, my roommate found my wallet as he was walking through the parking lot.

My roommate found my wallet, which was lying in plain sight right next to my car.

Dangling participles   A particular kind of misplaced participial phrase is the so-called dangling participle or dangler. The problem with these participles is not that they are located too far from the nouns they modify but that there is no appropriate noun anywhere in the vicinity to serve as an antecedent. The result is an abrupt shift of grammatical gears in midsentence.

Pacing nervously in the wings, the orchestra began the overture.

Turning to the second movement, a quiet introduction featuring a beautiful solo for the English horn leads to the main theme.

You see the problem. Who is pacing nervously in the wings? Surely not the orchestra—it's hard enough to play together sitting in one place. In the second sentence, the introduction is not turning to the second movement. The way to repair these sentences is either to supply an appropriate subject in the main clause for the participle to modify or to rewrite the phrase as a clause with its own subject.

Pacing nervously in the wings, the tenor heard the orchestra begin the overture.
As the tenor paced nervously in the wings, the orchestra began the overture.

Turning to the second movement, we hear [or "one hears"] a quiet introduction . . .
As we turn to the second movement, a quiet introduction . . .

A dangling participle may appear after the main clause as well as before, but it still needs a logical noun to modify. The following sentence appeared in a student's concert report.

> The "Stabat mater" is obviously a favorite text for composers to set, having heard Pergolesi's setting just last week.

Again there is no appropriate noun for the phrase to modify; the "Stabat mater" was not the one who heard Pergolesi last week. To correct this sentence, either supply an appropriate subject in the main clause or turn the modifying phrase into a clause.

> Having heard Pergolesi's setting just last week, I gather that the "Stabat mater" is a favorite text for composers to set.

> Since I heard Pergolesi's setting just last week, the 'Stabat mater" is obviously a favorite text for composers to set.

Like run-ons and sentence fragments, danglers result from sloppy thinking, flagging concentration, or some combination of the two.

Modifying clauses   Clauses that serve as modifiers, either adjectival or adverbial clauses, must also be located correctly in the sentence so that their modifying function is clear. Following is an example of a misplaced adverbial clause.

> When he was still very young, Mozart's father presented him at the Habsburg court.

The problem here is the pronoun in the subordinate clause, which must refer to the nearest antecedent, "Mozart's father." The way the sentence stands, Mozart's *father* was still very young when this happened; once again, the statement as it stands makes no sense. This sentence can be repaired by moving the clause, or better, by rearranging the nouns and pronouns so that the sentence makes sense. One might also distinguish between father and son by using their first names.

> Mozart's father presented him at the Habsburg court when he was still very young.

> When Mozart was still very young, his father presented him at the Habsburg court.

> When Wolfgang was still very young, Leopold presented him at the Habsburg court.

The way to clean up all types of misplaced modifiers is to back away from the sentence, think about what you are actually trying to say, and design a clearer way to say it. The answer to jumbled sentences like the incorrect examples above is not to add phrases or clauses in an attempt to clarify things, but to delete the jumble and start again, always with the basic idea in mind: Who is doing what to whom? Who is the subject, what is the action, and who or what is the object?

The Split Infinitive

Another problem of word order is the split infinitive. An old grammatical rule forbids splitting an infinitive, as in the following sentence.

> His goal in the symphonic poems was to as vividly as possible describe the main ideas or feelings depicted in the story.

The rule states that the infinitive—here, "to describe"—should not be interrupted by another word or phrase. The sentence should read as follows.

> His goal in the symphonic poems was to describe as vividly as possible . . .   OR
> . . . as vividly as possible to describe . . .

Some recent books on writing style allow the use of split infinitives, provided that only one word comes between the two parts of the infinitive, or if it seems the most graceful way to convey the thought. In formal papers, however, it is probably better to keep infinitives together in all situations. Deciding whether the modifying word or phrase should be placed before or after the infinitive ("to describe as vividly as possible" or "as vividly as possible to describe") is a question of choice. I think "to describe as vividly as possible" is smoother than the other choice, but both are correct.

Mixed Metaphors

Beyond the fairly cut-and-dried questions of correct grammar, one must consider questions of style in one's writing. Two perfectly correct sentences can vary widely in their force, elegance, and persuasive power, depending on variations in the style of the writing. In Chapter 7, we discussed stylistic issues such as word choice and sentence structure; here we want to single out one stylistic error that, like misplaced modifiers and danglers, creates an illogical or comic image—the mixed metaphor.

Metaphors are related to similes. A simile is a comparison between two realities, expressed using "like" or "as"; metaphors are comparisons expressed without "like" or "as."

> **Simile:** She sings like an angel. OR He tore through the finale like a man possessed.
>
> **Metaphor:** When the conductor humiliated me publicly, that was the last straw.

Both similes and metaphors can add color and elegance to your writing. "That was the last straw" is an economical and forceful substitute for "that was the deciding factor in my decision to quit." Problems arise when we forget that familiar expressions such as "last straw" or "light at the end of the tunnel" are not literal expressions but metaphors that create colorful pictures. We get into trouble when we try to extend metaphors too far or if we unwittingly mix incompatible metaphors. The so-called mixed metaphor confuses the reader by combining conflicting pictures. Think about the following sentences.

It was the sort of last-minute red herring on which an entire election can hinge.

The whole house of cards is built on sand.

Once he bit the bullet, rolled up his sleeves, and began practicing seriously, he could see the light at the end of the tunnel.

These sentences create startling, jarring pictures; readers are brought up short, bemused by the odd pictures, and the argument is momentarily derailed. The first two examples—the red herring and the house of cards— are taken from actual political rhetoric; I found both on the editorial pages of one of the country's great newspapers. It is difficult to suppress a smile when you read these gaffes; the writer's righteous indignation becomes funny rather than serious. If writers thought about what their metaphors were saying, they would not create these absurd mixtures.

When you venture into metaphor, be sure the comparison you choose is helpful rather than distracting, stay with a single comparison, be sure it does not get out of control, and abandon the comparison the instant it no longer serves your purpose.

SPELLING ISSUES

Using a Dictionary

English is a wondrous language, rich in vocabulary and synonyms, but it does have the disadvantage of illogical and inconsistent spelling. Study the following list of words, circle the ones that are misspelled, and write the correct spellings in the space at the right.

accommodate	liaison
anomaly	millennium
calendar	occasion
consensus	parallel
desperate	predilection
embarrassment	resistance
exhilarate	sacrilegious
fallacy	supersede
indispensable	tranquillity
judgment	weird

How many mistakes did you find? Actually, all these spellings are correct; check a reliable dictionary. The point was not to play a trick on you but to illustrate that English spelling is difficult. Even professional writers and editors keep a reliable dictionary handy and consult it frequently; you may have noticed as you studied the foregoing list that the longer you look at a word, the stranger it looks. Even small words look wrong if you stare at them long enough.

There are two ways to improve your spelling skills. The first is to accept the fact that spelling matters; unless you take correct spelling seriously, it will always seem random and impossible. Second, you have to own and use a good dictionary. No one expects every undergraduate student to own one of the oversize dictionaries that are standard in the world of publishing, such as *Webster's Third New International Dictionary*, but you need to own and use a good college dictionary, one of the standard hardbound dictionaries, such as *Merriam-Webster's Collegiate*, *American Heritage College*, *Random House Webster's College*, or *Webster's New World*. Note that dictionary titles sound similar and frequently contain the same names, such as Merriam and Webster. Choose your dictionary carefully and opt for a conservative one rather than one that lists all the latest slang usage. In any dictionary, when two spellings are listed for a word, assume that the first one is the standard and use it in your writing.

One group of words that students frequently misspell is adjectives and nouns derived from Latin participles. In American English, the final vowels in words like "predominant" and "occurrence" are all pronounced as *schwas* (an "uh" sound). Therefore, one cannot spell these words correctly simply by sounding them out. Since the choice of vowel depends on the conjugation of the Latin root, the only way to be sure of the spelling, short of learning Latin, is to look it up, and to continue to look it up, until you are sure of it.

Forming Possessives

The rule for forming possessives is this: Add an apostrophe and an "s" to form the possessive of a singular noun; add an apostrophe to form the possessive of plural nouns. An exception is plural words that end in letters other than "s," such as "women" and "children"; the plural of these words is formed by adding an apostrophe and "s." According to *The Chicago Manual of Style* (6.24–27), one should add an apostrophe and an "s" to proper nouns that end in "s" or another sibilant, except for "Jesus," "Moses," and any multisyllabic name with an unaccented ending pronounced "-eez," such as "Demosthenes" and "Sophocles." Thus, in current practice, the following possessives are correct.

Dickens's	Berlioz's	Euripides'
Marx's	Ives's	Jesus'
Burns's	Brahms's	Albéniz's

These possessives, though correct, look strange and sound awkward when you read them aloud. One can avoid the problem by rewriting the phrase.

the symphonies of Ives INSTEAD OF Ives's symphonies

the influence of Berlioz on later program music INSTEAD OF Berlioz's influence on later program music

Plurals of Borrowed Latin and Greek Words

Some students find it difficult to remember the singular and plural forms of borrowed Greek and Latin words; society at large has the same trouble. Writers forget, for instance, that "data" and "media" are the plural forms of "datum" and "medium," not singular nouns.

Wrong: The media has blown this problem all out of proportion.
Correct: The media have blown this problem all out of proportion.

Wrong: The data proves that lab rats prefer Mozart to Schoenberg.
Correct: The data prove that lab rats prefer Mozart to Schoenberg.

To use borrowed Latin and Greek words correctly, one must either memorize the correct form or consult a trustworthy dictionary. Following is a list of frequently misused borrowed Greek and Latin words, with their correct singular and plural forms.

Singular	Plural
addendum	addenda
alumnus (masculine)	alumni (masculine or mixed genders)
alumna (feminine)	alumnae (feminine)
crisis	crises
criterion	criteria
curriculum	curricula
datum	data
erratum	errata
medium	media
phenomenon	phenomena
thesis	theses

Foreign Words

Related to the issue of spelling is the question of correct treatment of foreign words. As a general rule, foreign words are set in italics unless they have become common English words. When foreign words are proper nouns or appear within quotation marks, as in a title, they need not be set in italics, since the quotation marks already set them off from the text.

Foreign words and names must be copied exactly as they appear in reference works, with all the appropriate accents, umlauts, tildes, and other diacritical marks. To omit any of these marks is to misspell the word or the name. It is no longer necessary to add these marks by hand; learn the proper commands and keystrokes to get your word-processing program to print them. Unless you have studied the foreign language in question, it is difficult to remember the exact nature and location of each accent mark, especially when you are dealing with Slavic names, such as Dvořák, or with long foreign titles, such as the French title of Debussy's *Prelude to the Afternoon of a Faun.* You should always consult a reliable reference work, such as the *New Grove* or the latest edition of *Baker's Biographical Dictionary,* and carefully follow the exact spellings found in those resources.

Recently, there have been changes in the standard ways of transliterating names from foreign alphabets. There is a new method of transliterating Chinese characters, so that we now write "Beijing" instead of "Peking." There have also been changes in the standard way of transliterating Russian names from the Cyrillic alphabet. One now sees spellings such as "Rakhmaninov," rather than the familiar Germanic spellings. It is always safe to follow the spellings found in standard reference works, provided that one follows them consistently. When a project focuses on a single composer or a few works, the writer quickly becomes accustomed to the correct spellings and accents of the names that occur constantly. One must rely on standard reference works and then be rigidly consistent in using one standard spelling.

Medieval and Renaissance Names

Some students have difficulty with the names of medieval and Renaissance personages, referring incorrectly to "da Vinci" or "de Vitry" as if those were family names. In those periods, people were often known by given name and place of origin, such as "Guillaume de Machaut," "Guido of Arezzo," and "Giovanni Pierluigi da Palestrina." They were also known by given name and an epithet, a description of something characteristic of them, such as "William the Conqueror" (known as "William the Bastard" before his victory in 1066), "Prince Henry the Navigator," "Richard Lionheart," "Notker the Stammerer," and "Charles the Bald." Compounding the confusion, medieval and Renaissance names are often translated into different languages, so that one can find many different versions of the same name. Petrus de Cruce, as he is known in Latin, is sometimes referred to as "Pierre de la Croix," and the Italian Trecento theorist is referred to as "Marchettus Padovensis," his Latin name, or "Marchetto da Padova" in Italian; a logical English translation would be "Marchetto of Padua." However you choose to refer to one of these personages, do not mix languages, like "Marchettus of Padova," and use the same form consistently.

Unfortunately, we have not been consistent in referring to these early figures, so that we commonly speak of "Machaut" as if that were the composer's last name, rather than the name of the town in which he was born. In library card catalogs, Machaut is alphabetized correctly under "G" for "Guillaume," whereas Palestrina is usually found incorrectly under "P." The only reason that we have been able to use "Machaut" and "Palestrina" as the names of these composers is that no one else of any historical importance ever came from those small towns. We certainly could not use the same system for other places, and write "Aquitaine" for William of Aquitaine or Eleanor, or use "Paris," "Rome," "Florence," or "London" as the names of specific persons.

When you are working on a project that involves names like these, consult a reliable reference work and be consistent in referring to them exactly as the sources do.

SOME TROUBLESOME WORD PAIRS

This section singles out for discussion a few pairs of similar words that are frequently confused in student papers.

Its and *It's*

It should not be difficult to distinguish these two tiny words and use them correctly. "Its," without an apostrophe, is the possessive form of the pronoun "it"; "it's," with the apostrophe, is a contraction of "it is." A common error is to use "it's" to indicate possession, probably because we associate the apostrophe with possession.

Wrong: The committee will announce it's decision on Monday.

Correct: The committee will announce its decision on Monday.

Just remember that "its" is the possessive pronoun. "It's," the contraction, would seldom be appropriate in a formal paper, since contractions are out of place in that context.

Your and *You're*

A similar situation exists with these two words. "Your," without the apostrophe, is the possessive form of the second-person pronoun; "you're," with the apostrophe, is a contraction of "you are." The common error is to use "you're" to indicate possession, again probably because of the association of the apostrophe with possession. "You're," the contraction, is not likely to be appropriate in a formal paper.

Wrong: You're version of the theme was too slow.

Correct: Your version of the theme was too slow.

Whose and Who's

"Whose" is the possessive form of the relative pronoun "who"; "who's" is a contraction of "who is." The common mistake, as in the two previous cases, is to write the contraction instead of the correct possessive. Once again, awareness that contractions are generally out of place in a formal paper will help you to avoid these errors.

Wrong: Leonard Bernstein, who's works span a wide variety of genres and styles . . .

Correct: Leonard Bernstein, whose works span a wide variety . . .

Affect and Effect

These two similar words cause great confusion for writers. Put as simply as possible, "affect" is generally a verb meaning "to produce an effect or change." It also can be used as a noun meaning an emotion. "Effect" is generally a noun meaning "the result, consequence, or outcome of something." It can also be used as a verb meaning "to achieve or bring about." In the following sentences, the two words are used correctly.

Her performance affected me greatly.

The effect of her solo was startling.

Music is a powerful way to portray affects like love and yearning.

If the committee manages to effect the removal of that requirement, the effect on the school will be enormous.

Due to and Because of

Student writers often confuse "due to" and "because of." "Due" is an adjective, not a conjunction; therefore, "due to" can be correctly used only after some form of the verb "to be," as a predicate adjective. "Due to" is not correct at the beginning of a sentence.

Wrong: Due to the troubled political climate in Italy, Verdi constantly had trouble with the Austrian censors.

Correct: Because of the troubled political climate in Italy, Verdi constantly had trouble with the Austrian censors.

Correct: Verdi's constant trouble with the Austrian censors was due to the troubled political climate in Italy.

Discreet and Discrete

These two adjectives sound the same but mean completely different things. "Discreet" means "prudent, tactful, or careful," and "discrete" means "separate or individual." In the following sentences, the words are used correctly.

Committees that deal with personnel matters need to be discreet.

His creative life can be divided into three discrete phases.

Instead of four discrete movements, this symphony is organized as a unified work in five connected sections.

Fewer and Less

"Fewer" and "less" are both antonyms of "more." "Fewer" means a smaller number of individual, countable things; "less" means a smaller quantity of a single thing. The common error is to use "less" instead of "fewer" to apply to individual things.

Wrong: The band would sound better with less clarinets.

Correct: The band would sound better if there were fewer clarinets.

Correct: That soprano would sound better with less vibrato.

Principal and Principle

"Principal" is generally an adjective meaning "main" or "most important," although it also can be used as a noun meaning "the head of a school" or "an amount of money." "Principle" is a noun meaning "a fundamental law or doctrine." In the following sentences, the two words are used correctly.

The new principal horn of the Philharmonic is Ignaz Feuermann.

The new principal of the high school has greatly improved the music program.

A good essay must be based on the principles of unity and coherence.

He is a man of principle.

The discussion of troublesome pairs of words could go on much longer; we have discussed only a few common errors. Consult one of the style guides for further details. All these issues go back to a principle we discussed earlier: The writer should treat words with respect and choose them carefully, conscious of their meaning and import.

PUNCTUATION

Correct punctuation is another troublesome area for many student writers. Consult Chapter 5 of *The Chicago Manual of Style* or Part VI of the *Simon & Schuster Handbook* for authoritative discussions of the proper use of punctuation. Here I will mention a few situations that seem to cause problems for students.

The Period

The period is used after every complete sentence. It is also used after abbreviations, such as "m." for "measure," "mm." for "measures," and "ms." for "manuscript." All footnotes end with a period. In bibliography entries, a period appears between the author's name and the title, between the title and the publication information, and at the end of the entry. See Chapter 5 for discussion of the proper format for footnotes and bibliographies.

In a typed paper, it is accepted practice to put a space after every period, particularly after periods that follow abbreviations. Thus "m.5" and "mm.15–22" are incorrect, since there are no spaces following the periods; these should be typed as "m. 5" and "mm. 15–22." There should also be a space after the period following an initial in a name—thus, "J. S. Bach," *not* "J.S.Bach." One exception to this rule is academic degrees, which do not include spaces—thus, "B.A.," "M.A.," "M.M.," "D.M.A.," and "Ph.D."

Note: Many of us were trained to double-space after a period or any other punctuation mark at the end of a sentence. That practice is falling into disuse; the usual explanation is that that extra space is not necessary, now that most fonts have proportional spacing. There still are situations when I think the extra space is an improvement, for instance at the end of a sentence that ends with a quotation followed by a period, quotation marks, and a footnote number. At this point it seems to be a matter of choice or the writer's preference. Whatever you choose to do, you must do it consistently throughout the paper.

The Comma

Many student writers seem mystified by the comma. Some situations are particularly troublesome.

Series In a series containing more than two items, commas should separate each item from the other, including the last one.

> The leading composers of the Mannheim school were Johann Stamitz, Ignaz Holzbauer, Christian Cannabich, and Carl Stamitz.

Some style guides now allow the omission of the last comma, before "and," provided that a comma is not required for clarity. That style of punctuating a series is common in journalistic writing but not in scholarly papers; *The Chicago Manual of Style* (5.57) requires the inclusion of that final comma. If one chooses to omit it, there is always the danger that the last two items will be read as a two-part single item, such as Gilbert and Sullivan or Rodgers and Hammerstein.

Appositives If a phrase simply tells us something more about a noun, rather than making a general noun more specific, it should be set off by commas.

Monteverdi's *Orfeo,* an opera in the Florentine style, was first performed in 1607.

If an appositive phrase is restrictive—that is, if it makes a general noun specific—then commas are not used.

Verdi's opera *La Traviata* is based on a novel by Dumas.

If commas were used to set off the title in that last sentence, the sentence would imply that *La Traviata* was the only opera Verdi composed.

Restrictive and nonrestrictive clauses   Commas are used to set off nonrestrictive clauses, just as they are used to set off nonrestrictive appositives; commas are not used to set off restrictive clauses.

Arnold Schoenberg, who fled from Nazi Germany in the thirties, . . .

The composers who fled from Nazi Germany in the thirties . . .

In the first sentence, the relative clause is nonrestrictive; it adds information rather than making a general subject more specific, since we already know exactly who the subject is. Therefore, commas must be used. In the second sentence, the relative clause is restrictive, making the general noun "composers" more specific; the clause answers the question "Which composers?" Therefore, commas are not used.

Compound and complex sentences   A comma is used between the clauses of a compound sentence, provided that they are joined by a conjunction. If the clauses are short and there is no possibility of confusion, the comma may be omitted.

Berg used the twelve-tone system freely to create a style we usually describe as expressionist, but Webern extended the twelve-tone idea into new areas.

A comma is used between the clauses of complex sentences.

Although much of the music of the postwar period can be traced to the influence of Webern, the neoromanticism of recent years can be interpreted as a return to the freer and more expressive style of Berg.

Introductory phrases   A comma is generally used after all introductory phrases. If the introductory phrase is short and there is no possibility of misinterpretation, the comma may be omitted. Both the following sentences are punctuated correctly.

Judging from the correspondence, we can conclude that Brahms was very worried about the first performance of his First Symphony.

In 1723 Bach accepted the post of Cantor at the Thomaskirche in Leipzig.

In the case of a short introductory phrase, if there is any possibility of confusion or what the *Chicago Manual* calls "mistaken junction," the comma should be included to ensure clarity.

Confusing: Soon after the concert was interrupted by loud catcalls and angry denunciations.

Clear: Soon after, the concert was interrupted by loud catcalls and angry denunciations.

Without the comma, the eye sees "after the concert" as a prepositional phrase, confusing the reader.

Commas are also used in the following situations.

In titles, dates, and numbers:
Friday, September 4, 1596; 425,000.

To set off parenthetical elements, interjections, and words of direct address:
Bach, it is believed, was born on March 21.

The evidence, dear reader, supports my conclusion.

To separate complementary or antithetical elements:
Bach's harsh, though at the same time brilliant, criticism was not lost on the town council.

To separate elements forming a confusing conjunction:
To Gilbert, Sullivan was an enigma.

In elliptical constructions to indicate omission:
Beethoven wrote nine symphonies; Brahms, four.

The Semicolon

The semicolon marks a more important break in the flow of a sentence than breaks marked by a comma. In particular, the semicolon is used to separate the two parts of a compound sentence when they are not connected by a conjunction.

Stravinsky performed as a pianist and conductor all his life; Schoenberg was a university teacher.

Note: Words such as "however," "still," "yet," and "hence" are adverbs, not conjunctions. Therefore, if the second clause starts with one of these words, a comma is not sufficient punctuation between the clauses; a semicolon is necessary. As an alternative, one can rewrite the sentence as two separate sentences.

Wrong: Stravinsky performed as a pianist and conductor all his life, however Schoenberg was a university professor.

Correct: Stravinsky performed as a pianist and conductor all his life; Schoenberg, however, was a university professor.

Correct: Stravinsky performed as a pianist and conductor all his life. Schoenberg, however, was a university professor.

When items in a series are long and complex, and when they contain internal commas, semicolons are used to separate the items.

> Among Verdi's most popular works are *Rigoletto,* produced in Venice in 1851; *La Traviata,* produced in Venice in 1853; and *Aïda,* produced in Cairo in 1871.

The Colon

The colon is used to mark a greater break in the flow of a sentence than breaks marked by the semicolon. In expository prose, the colon has two main uses. The first is to introduce a formal statement or quotation; the second is to introduce a list.

> The rule may be stated thus: Material that appeared in the dominant or in another related key in the exposition returns in the tonic in the recapitulation.
>
> He answered as follows: No prince may force me to compose at his whim.
>
> Rosen's book deals with the composers whom he views as the chief exponents of the Classical style: Haydn, Mozart, and Beethoven.

Quotation Marks

Chapter 5 discussed the proper format for brief and long quotations and the conventions one should follow when citing the words of someone else. You may want to review that section. Here we need to add a few rules about quotation marks in combination with other kinds of punctuation. Note that American practice diverges from British practice in this matter; we are concerned with American practice.

1. Periods and commas required by the context of the sentence are placed inside the quotation marks, whether or not the period or the comma is part of the quoted material. The following sentences are correctly punctuated.

> At the conclusion of "Sempre libera," we know much more about Violetta's character and her ambivalence about love.
>
> A striking example of Ives's technique of quotation is "Decoration Day."

This rule seems to cause more objections and discussions than any other. What bothers students is that the comma is not part of the quoted title, any more than the period is part of the title of "Decoration Day." Nevertheless, in the United States those punctuation marks are placed inside the quotation marks. Period.

2. Semicolons, colons, question marks, and exclamation points required by the context of the sentence are placed outside quotation marks. Thus:

> A good example of his collage technique is "Decoration Day"; a clear example of his impressionist style is "The Housatonic at Stockbridge."

The only difference between these two clauses is that they end with different punctuation marks; the semicolon after the first clause goes outside the quotation marks; the period at the end goes inside. It may seem illogical, but that is how it is done in the United States.

The Hyphen

The hyphen is used to divide the first part of a word at the end of a line from the second part at the beginning of the next line. Students frequently err in the way they divide words. Short or one-syllable words should not be divided at all; longer words may be divided, provided that you follow the rules for dividing words correctly. Consult a dictionary to check the proper division of words, or keep the word together and start it on the next line.

Hyphens are also used in compound constructions such as "two-voice," "one-syllable," "well-read," and "long-neglected," when they function as adjectives and appear before the nouns they modify. Generally, compounds are not hyphenated when they appear as predicate adjectives at the end of the sentence.

A well-read person would not make a glaring mistake like that.

I like talking with him because he is well read.

It is impossible to keep straight in your mind which compounds are hyphenated and which are written as one word or as two words. Accepted practice seems to be moving in the direction of using fewer hyphens; "lowercase," "neoclassical," and "nonconformist," for example, are standard. Consult a dictionary if you are unsure whether a compound should be hyphenated. Even if standard usage does not require a hyphen, it may be necessary to use one in some situations to avoid confusion.

The so-called suspended hyphen can be used in compound constructions, but it can be confusing and should be used with great care. It is correct to write "in three- and four-voice polyphony," or "four-, five-, and "six-voice madrigals," meaning "in three-voice and four-voice polyphony," and "madrigals for four, five, and six voices," but be careful that your meaning is clear and your punctuation is correct.

On most keyboards, a hyphen is also used to indicate ranges of numbers, as in "pp. 45-48" or "1984-87." Printers use a small dash, called an "en dash," larger than a hyphen and smaller than a regular dash, for that purpose. If your program allows that, fine; otherwise, use a hyphen.

The Dash

Dashes can be used in expository prose to interrupt a sentence's structure to add information, such as a definition, an explanation, or a reaction or comment. Although this construction should be used with restraint, it can be effective.

The composers of the late madrigal—Marenzio, Monteverdi, and Gesualdo—based their musical style on rhetorical effects.

There are several other ways to convey that idea without using the dashes. Note also that on most keyboards now, you can form a continuous dash rather than two hyphens; note also that no space appears before or after the dash.

Parentheses

Parentheses are used to enclose additional information that breaks up the flow of the sentence. The most common error regarding parentheses is to overuse them. If the material is important, it deserves to be included somehow in the text without parentheses. If it is not important, then it should not be included in the text—leave it out or put it in a footnote. Constant use of parentheses means that the writer has not thought out clearly what he or she wants to say; parentheses thus become a way to fit in last-minute additions and afterthoughts.

There are many other rules and details about punctuation. There is no need to discuss exclamation points here, since they are of little use in expository prose. Experience with student papers shows that the most critical need is for students to learn the correct use of the comma. For further details of correct punctuation, consult Chapter 5 of *The Chicago Manual of Style*, Chapter 3 of the Turabian guide, or Part VI of the *Simon & Schuster Handbook for Writers*.

SPECIAL PROBLEMS INVOLVED IN WRITING ABOUT MUSIC

Technical Terms

Every field of study has its own vocabulary of technical terms. We need these terms so that we can describe the phenomena under discussion with accuracy and precision, and so that readers can understand exactly what we are trying to say. If we did not have terms such as "sonata-allegro form," "Wagner style," or "impressionism," we would have to write whole paragraphs describing what they mean. To use this powerful means of communication effectively, we should be aware of some guidelines for the use of technical terms.

Using technical terms correctly   First, treat technical terms with respect, and use them carefully. Each term, like any other word, has its own particular force and connotation, and the writer should use that term only when that precise force and connotation is appropriate. There are several terms, for instance, that can be used to describe a polyphonic texture: imitation, canon, fugue, fugato, stretto, and so on. These terms are not interchangeable; each has its own special shade of meaning, and, if the writer carelessly uses them as if they were synonyms, the reader will not get a true impression of what the writer is trying to say. Like all words, technical terms are powerful tools that should be used with care and respect.

Second, choose standard technical terms; do not try to make up new ones. Sometimes students coin ungainly new terms to describe musical phenomena; one sees phrases such as "a fugue-type texture," or "a sonata-like structure." In the first instance, the student probably means "an imitative texture" or "a polyphonic texture." The standard terms are much clearer and infinitely more elegant than any awkward, newly invented pseudoterms.

Third, be careful about anachronistic use of technical terms. An *anachronism* is something inappropriate for the time under discussion; it would be an anachronism if, in a production of *Romeo and Juliet,* Romeo pulled a cell phone from his pocket in the middle of the balcony scene. Anachronistic terminology frequently appears in students' discussions of early music; some students use the term "fugal" to describe imitative writing in Renaissance Masses and motets. Not only does "fugal" mean something different from the compositional practice in question, but also "fugue" as a technical term refers to eighteenth-century musical practice and is inappropriate in discussions of Renaissance music. Other obvious examples of anachronistic use of technical terms would be writing about secondary dominants in Machaut motets, modulation from key to key in Gesualdo motets, or, moving in the opposite direction, isorhythm in Stravinsky's Mass. It takes work to uncover complex ways of organizing and relating musical events in a composition; it also takes care and precision to find or choose the appropriate term to describe what you see going on.

Finally, as we mentioned in Chapter 7, once you use a word as a technical term, it is no longer available for use in its general, nontechnical sense; you cannot use the term in both senses.

Genre, form, and style Musicological writings regularly use some general terms to express the nature and characteristics of the music under discussion. Among these terms are genre, form, and style, three important terms that overlap to some extent but actually represent distinct points of view in regard to musical works. Because there is some overlap, unfortunately one can find examples in which writers use them almost as synonyms; no wonder students have some difficulty using the terms precisely and convincingly in their writings. Let me try to make clear the distinctions among these terms.

Genre is a general term for the category or kind of musical work represented by the example under discussion; examples of genres are "symphony," "motet," "concerto," and "opera." Genres are generally very inclusive terms;

the genre "symphony" includes works as diverse as Haydn's *Drum-roll*, Beethoven's Ninth, Bruckner's Seventh, Mahler's *Resurrection* Symphony, and Stravinsky's Symphony in Three Movements, among hundreds of others. "Symphony" does not imply a specific form, unless the context makes clear that the writer is talking about a group of similar works, such as Mozart symphonies. Even then, although there may be formal or stylistic implications associated with the term, the fact that an individual work departs from the standard expectations does not mean that it is not a symphony. Other inclusive genres include "opera," a term that includes works as diverse as *Orfeo*, *Giulio Cesare, Don Giovanni, Salome*, and *Nixon in China*, and "Mass," which includes works by, for example, Josquin des Prez, Bach, Mozart, Beethoven, and Stravinsky. On the other hand, some genres are confined to a narrower time period, and therefore connote more details about matters of form and style. An example of that sort of genre is "ballata," nearly always used for Italian Trecento vocal pieces in a particular form—*AbbaA*, like the virelai. Still, as a genre, the term first and foremost connotes a category of music, not a form or a style.

Form, our term for the way musical ideas are organized to create coherent larger compositions, seems to be a more straightforward concept than "genre" or "style." "Form" implies something observable, quantifiable. We regard terms such as "sonata-allegro form," "rondo," "fugue," "theme and variations," "strophic form," and "ritornello form" as clear and definite, standing for a specific pattern that either is or is not present in a few pages of score. But even here, things are not always that clear. "Sonata-allegro" and "fugue," for example, are often described as processes rather than specific forms. In addition, a term such as "sonata-allegro form" can be applied to vastly diverse musical works; although we associate the term first with Mozart and Haydn, Tchaikovsky's *Romeo and Juliet* Overture can be analyzed as a huge, overblown sonata-allegro structure, whose slow introduction is five minutes long, as long as the entire first movement of a typical Classical symphony. Although we often use the term "rondo" as an abstract formal term for any structure we can diagram as *ABACA* or *ABACABA*, no matter what the period or style is, the term has always carried connotations of a dance form, a lighthearted romp, suitable for the finale of a symphony or a concerto. Even the concept of form is not as simple as it might seem, but form seems to be easier to grasp than the cloudier concepts of genre and style.

Style refers to the specific characteristics of a piece of music that give it its specific identity. "Style" embraces the details of every facet of a musical work—its melodic contours, rhythm and meter, articulation, harmonic vocabulary, instrumentation, and so forth. The concept of style is what we use to identify and understand a musical work as we listen to it; the term embraces the details that we identify and process to create a mental picture of the music. In addition, the term "style" is connected with the general concept of "stylistic periods," such as Renaissance, Baroque, Classical, and Romantic. "Baroque," if you think about it, cannot possibly be a term for a single style, since, like any arbitrary historical construct, the period we call the Baroque era embraces works as stylistically diverse as monodies by Monteverdi and Rossi, polychoral motets by Schütz, experimental violin sonatas by Biagio Marini, Lully operas, Handel oratorios, and Bach concertos.

Perhaps an example will help clarify the distinctions among these three terms. Let us imagine that you are looking at the first movement of a Haydn string quartet. The genre of this piece, in the broadest sense, is "chamber music," as opposed to orchestral music, solo vocal music, piano music, choral music, and so on; the specific genre, of course, is "string quartet." Like the other terms for genres I mentioned, "string quartet" is a very inclusive term, including works as diverse as quartets by Mozart, Beethoven, and Bartók. The correct term for the form of Haydn's first movement is probably "sonata-allegro form," but it might be "sonata-rondo" or some other form; you have to read through the score and determine the form yourself to be sure. The style of the movement embraces all the musical details—the nature of the melodic ideas, meter and rhythm, the interplay between the four instruments, the harmonic language, and so on. In a listening exam, the stylistic details are the evidence you use to identify the genre, form, and general style of the piece.

Keep these concepts clear in your head; knowing how these three related but distinct terms are used will help to clarify your thinking about musical works; using them correctly will help establish your understanding of music and your ability to discuss it intelligently.

Describing Musical Events

In Chapter 1, I pointed out that it is not easy to describe musical events. Finding a clear way of expressing what occurs in a musical work is sometimes a difficult challenge. Three particular questions deserve discussion.

Point of view: Subjects and verbs   One area to consider carefully is how to describe what happens in a musical work. If you want to describe a striking cadenza in a violin concerto, for example, there are several ways of stating your idea. Consider the following sentences.

> The solo violin embarks on a brilliant exploration of motives taken from the first theme.

> The composer turns the soloist loose in a brilliant cadenza based on motives taken from the first theme.

> Motives taken from the first theme are woven into a brilliant cadenza.

None of these descriptions is completely satisfactory. The first seems to ascribe the cadenza to the instrument rather than to the composer or the soloist; the second overpersonalizes the interaction between composer and interpreter; the third falls into the passive voice. Perhaps the following versions are more suitable.

> A brilliant cadenza for the soloist continues to explore motives taken from the first theme.
>
> The soloist then plays a brilliant cadenza based on motives taken from the first theme.

Experiment with several versions of musical description until you find one that avoids the multiple pitfalls of pretentious language, overly personal description, and weak passive-voice constructions.

Point of view: Tenses   It is not always easy to choose the proper tense of the verbs when describing musical events. In general, the present tense is appropriate when the reader's attention is focused on the music itself. If the emphasis is on the composer's act of creating the music or on the details of a particular performance, the past tense is appropriate. Consider the verb tenses in the following sentences.

> In the opening chorus of Cantata No. 4, the sopranos sing the chorale melody in long notes, while the other voices sing free counterpoint.
>
> In the opening chorus of Cantata No. 4, Bach assigned the chorale tune to the sopranos and composed free counterpoint for the other voices.
>
> At the end of the coda, the brass section repeats the main theme once more, bringing this long movement to a dramatic conclusion.
>
> In typical Romantic fashion, Liszt chose to restate the main theme once more at the end of the coda, assigning it to the brass section.

One reads statements like "Bach assigns the chorale tune to the sopranos," but that wording is jarring—after all, Bach died a long time ago. Even when you are describing ongoing or repeated actions that took place in the past, the past tense makes better sense than the present.

> Schubert consistently chose the texts for his songs from the works of a few favorite poets.
>
> Bach based many of his cantatas on the chorale tunes that had been traditional in the Lutheran church for two hundred years.

Another error is to use present and past tenses in the same sentence or paragraph. If you start by using the present tense, choosing as your point of view the style and organization of the music rather than the composer's creative choices, stay with that point of view and that tense. Constant vacillation between present and past tense is confusing.

Finding appropriate ways to state qualitative judgments   Another challenge in writing about music, or any art, is finding appropriate ways to state qualitative judgments. It is not enough for the writer to label everything "beautiful." The writer must search through the huge store of synonyms in the English language to find the exact word that says what he or she wants to say. The weakest possible critical term is "interesting"; that is what one mumbles when standing, baffled, in front of the latest avant-garde painting or installation. "Stirring," "ravishing," "majestic," "eerie," or "chilling" might be appropriate to describe late Romantic works, but they might be entirely inappropriate to characterize Renaissance music or some of the more abstract and cerebral styles of twentieth-century music. On the other hand, "challenging," "intriguing," "tightly organized," or "cerebral" may work to describe modernistic music but are not the correct terms for late Romantic tone poems.

It takes thought and creativity to come up with exactly the right word to describe the aesthetic effect of a particular piece of music. One wants to avoid both extremes—dull words like "interesting," and affected or pretentious language. Finding the right evaluative word to use in your summary or conclusion may seem to be the most difficult part of writing a paper, but it is worth the struggle to find the one word that will say exactly what you want to say and provide a strong, effective conclusion.

SUMMARY

This chapter has discussed some problems that mar student writing in any field, along with some of the special difficulties of writing about music. The advice is intended to provide practical assistance; if you approach your writing assignments armed with an awareness of common writing errors and ways to avoid them, your task should be easier. You should be able to write and edit your assignments with a greater sense of security, confident that your papers are more likely to be taken seriously as representative of the high quality of your work.

Conclusion

Since the purpose of this book is to provide practical advice about writing research papers and other projects on musical topics, the emphasis in the second half of the book has been on the mechanics and technical details of writing. Although they may seem minor, these details are important; treating them carelessly can defeat the writer's goal of conveying his or her ideas to the reader. The unifying theme of this book, running through all the discussions of details, is that effective writing takes time, care, and precision. Each step in the process of writing a paper—research, drafting, editing, printing, and proofreading—demands that the writer understand each specific task and expend the necessary time and effort to do things in the proper way. To succeed as a writer, you must take sufficient pride in your work to care about technical matters such as proper format, correct spelling, and careful editing. Students will never succeed in their writing assignments until they develop a competent and professional prose style.

It is time now to step back from the details and return to the larger perspective with which the book began. Effective and careful writing can vastly improve a paper, and an incompetent and careless writing style can lessen or even destroy the effectiveness of a paper. Important as it is to develop a competent and effective writing style, however, a good writing style is not enough in itself to produce effective prose about music. The ability to write clear, effective prose is only a means of communicating the writer's insight and vision about the art of music. To write well about music, the writer needs two things: vision and insight about music, and the writing skill to communicate that vision clearly and effectively. Unless the writer has the analytical skills to understand a musical work, the aesthetic sensitivity to appreciate its beauty, the historical insight to understand its significance in the history of music, and the awareness to see how it relates to cultural issues, all the writing skill in the world will not produce prose worth reading. Even an understanding of music and its history is not enough to produce a good paper; one also needs the imagination and creativity to design a thesis or point of view that connects all the data into a unified, forceful statement. One needs to have both something to say and the skill to say it clearly and forcefully. I have presumed throughout this book that the student writer has something to say; my mission has been to provide practical assistance in the craft of saying it clearly.

I close with a plea to all students: Read as many books and articles about music as you can. Read voraciously. After you read the books and articles that are required in connection with your classes, read everything else you can. Read widely but critically, with one eye on the content and the other on the writing style. When you come across a writer whose style impresses you with its clarity and eloquence, find other writings by the same author, no matter what the subject, so that you can study what makes that writer's style effective. Find models that impress you, and try to isolate exactly what it is about the writer's skill that makes it so clear and enjoyable to read. Learn from all your reading, and continue to read with an eye on writing style, looking for ways to improve the clarity and effectiveness of your own writing. Improving your writing is a lifelong task, one that is never finished, but every effort to improve it, even in a small way, will make your writing more effective and your schoolwork more successful.

A P P E N D I X

Sample Paper

The third edition of this guide closes, as the earlier editions did, with a sample paper, an example of how all the matters discussed in the book come together to create an interesting and convincing research paper. This is a real research paper by a real student; it is reprinted here with the writer's permission. Read this paper carefully, taking note not only of what the writer is saying—the topic, thesis, and argumentation—but also of how he says it. This writer exercised exemplary care and precision in dealing with every phase of the process: research, organization, writing, editing, footnotes, bibliography, and format issues.

I like everything about this paper. I think the topic is creative and thought-provoking; it is always fascinating to glimpse the inner working of the creative process and the collaboration between a writer and a composer. In addition, the writer has a definite thesis, which he argues convincingly, relying on his thorough control of the literature about these important artists and solid analysis of the music. He raises questions that pique our curiosity and defends his viewpoint on these questions with authority. His bibliography is remarkably extensive for a paper of this size, and he uses his sources well.

Close study of this paper would make a useful class project; it also would be a good exercise for you to undertake on your own. After scanning the paper quickly to get a general sense of the topic, thesis, and arguments, go over the paper carefully, page by page, sentence by sentence, trying to grasp how the writer dealt with the various issues and processes involved in writing. The following questions should help to guide your analysis of the paper.

1. What is the exact *topic* of this paper? Does the title accurately reflect what the actual topic is, or did it create expectations in your mind that were not met in the paper?

2. What is the *thesis* of this paper? Remember, the thesis is the topic sentence of the entire paper; it has to be a sentence, not just a couple of words or a phrase. Find the one sentence in the paper that you think states the thesis most clearly. Exactly where does this sentence appear in the paper? Does it appear early enough to guide the reader's thoughts? Too early? Too late? Are there several different sentences that you might single out as the best statement of the thesis?

3. List the main *arguments* the writer uses to defend his thesis, stating them in complete sentences. Are there any arguments that are not explained or defended sufficiently? Are the arguments discussed one by one, or do ideas from one argument bleed into another? Does the writer let you know when he is moving from one argument to another? Is the logical progression of his thought easy for the reader to follow?

4. Are there ideas that require more explanation? Does the writer assume too much prior knowledge in the reader? Do you understand his ideas and arguments, or do you feel left in the dark about anything?

5. Do you think he added anything to your ideas about the topic, or did he simply rehash familiar ideas and approaches? Did you feel that his arguments were convincing?

6. How about the *tone* of his language? Did he use too many technical terms or big words for you? Did he seem focused on arguing his ideas forcefully, or on establishing his knowledge of arcane facts?

7. Does the *introduction* lead smoothly into the topic, or did you feel it was either too short or too long? Does it contain ideas that you think need more explanation?

8. Does the *conclusion,* in your opinion, wrap up the whole project gracefully and convincingly? Did it leave you with the feeling that you would like to know more about this fascinating topic?

9. Look again at his *musical examples.* Were they well chosen? Was the point of each example clear? Did they advance his arguments effectively?

10. Finally, discuss your general reaction to the paper in a paragraph or two. How would you grade it, compared with other examples of student prose you have read? Would you call this writer a good writer? Is there anything you would change? In your opinion, are there sections of the paper that need to be expanded or shortened? If you were the professor grading this paper, what grade would you assign to it?

I could give you my own answers to these questions, but the point of the exercise is for you to develop your own critical skills. As I already said, I consider this a model paper, a fine example of what first-rate student writers can achieve. I should explain one potential problem that I hope you noticed; the writer refers to the complex philosophical notion of word and deed in Goethe's *Faust* in one short introductory sentence and then moves immediately into his discussion of Strauss and Hofmannsthal. You may have singled that sentence out as an example of an important concept that needs more explanation, or perhaps you felt the need for a longer introduction. There is a reason for this brief reference. The paper was written for a class that had spent a great deal of time discussing Goethe's *Faust* and its influence on nineteenth-century literature and music; in this context, an elaborate explanation of the concept of word and deed in *Faust* was not necessary. Other than that one thing, this paper is a fine model, one that you would do well to imitate in matters of argumentation, style, and format, as well as in general approach.

Finally, bear in kind that the process of analyzing prose about music is the same whether you are reading a book, an article from one of the journals, or a student paper. Think of this same list of questions whenever you are reading expository prose about music or any other topic; reread a journal article that impressed you and ask those same questions. The more you try to take apart good prose, extracting the topic, thesis, and arguments, checking the outline, asking yourself whether the arguments are clear and convincing, thinking about the level and tone of the language, judging the effectiveness of the introduction and conclusion, and looking at details of format, the better you will understand the writing process and the more ways you will find to improve your own writing. Read everything you can, and read analytically, questioning the organization, content, language, and format of what you read. The best way to improve your writing is to read voraciously, read critically, and try to incorporate the good qualities of what you read into your own writing.

ECHOES OF *FAUST:*
Word versus Deed in the
Recognition Scene of *Elektra*

Andrew Whitfield
MUS 896
May 3, 1999

When he addressed the question of word vs. deed in *Faust*,[1] Johann Wolfgang von Goethe (1749–1832) raised an aesthetic dilemma that echoed throughout the nineteenth century. This dichotomy also represented a crucial factor in the artistic collaboration of Hugo von Hofmannsthal (1874–1929) and Richard Strauss (1864–1949), a relationship which officially began in 1906, when Strauss consented to set Hofmannsthal's drama *Elektra* to music. Although Hofmannsthal's free adaptation of Sophocles offers remarkably complex psychological characterizations, its plot centers on Elektra's obsession with the *deed* of revenge. Strauss telescoped Hofmannsthal's drama as much as possible because he "knew instinctively how important it was to reduce a text to its essentials in order to produce a good opera text."[2] Yet despite these exhaustive cuts, Strauss asked for additional text from Hofmannsthal when he needed more *words* in order to attain his musical goal. This paper will examine the ways in which the dramatic ideal and the musical ideal are affected by Strauss's musical and textual insertions in one of these key moments, the scene of recognition between Elektra and Orestes.

In order to understand the nature of Hofmannsthal's drama, one must first consider the defining aesthetic factors that governed Hofmannsthal's creativity in *fin-de-siècle* Vienna. Hofmannsthal began his literary career in

---

[1] See Goethe's *Faust,* I: 1224–1237, where Faust is translating the opening line of the Gospel of John. In the Norton Critical Edition translation by Walter Arndt, Faust ultimately renders "In the beginning was the Word" as "In the beginning was the Deed."

[2] Bryan Gilliam, *Richard Strauss's Elektra* (Oxford: Clarendon Press, 1991), 36.

Vienna as a poet at the age of seventeen, "quickly absorbing the fashionable poetic and plastic culture of all Europe."[3] The problem with this aesthetic direction for Hofmannsthal was that it felt too narcissistic and too solipsistic; the poet, who has a great dependency on and love for fashionable *words,* was condemned to seek the meaning of life "purely within his own psyche."[4] This meant that the poet's words would gradually cease to reflect human experience. Although the society that favored his poetry seemed perfectly content to live in this artistic "prison," Hofmannsthal rejected the notion of art as separate from society. According to Bryan Gilliam, "Hofmannsthal sought to forge connections between art and experience, between the individual and civilization."[5] Ultimately, Hofmannsthal recognized the potential for art to awaken the human instinct. Through an affirmation of the instinctual, the artist would then be released from his own psyche, and "the door to the life of action and society" would be opened again.[6]

It was at this point in his career that Hofmannsthal focused his attention on drama, and *Elektra* represents Hofmannsthal's first foray into this new artistic genre.[7] Although Hofmannsthal admired the fusion of the arts in theatre, the real importance of the medium was its use of gesture (as opposed to the *words* alone of poetry) as a means of expression. "A

[3] Carl E. Schorske, *Fin-de-Siècle Vienna: Politics and Culture* (New York: Vintage Books, 1981), pp. 15–16.
[4] Schorske, 16.
[5] Gilliam, 21.
[6] Schorske, 19.
[7] Gilliam, 23.

pure gesture is pure thought . . . in pure gestures the true personality
comes to light," observed Hofmannsthal in his 1911 essay *On
Pantomime.*[8] For Hofmannsthal, words did not maintain this purity of
gesture; they tended to "generalize rather than reveal pure thought."[9] This
interest in gesture led Hofmannsthal to favor mythic subjects "reworked
with a contemporary sensibility."[10] In the preface to *Die Ägyptische
Helena,* Hofmannsthal defended his preference for mythological subjects:

> If this age of ours is anything, it is mythical—I know of no
> other expression for an existence that unfolds in the face of
> such vast horizons—for this being surrounded by millennia . . .
> for this immense inner breadth, these mad inner tensions. . . . It
> is impossible to catch all this in middle-class dialogue. Let us
> write mythological operas! Believe me they are the truest of all
> forms.[11]

Thus, for Hofmannsthal, the power of a mythological subject, such as
Elektra, lay in its potential for the truest gesture contained in the truest
form; furthermore, such an absolute gesture is the product not of words,
but of action ("the *deed.*") Gilliam observes that this division between
"language and gesture—between word and deed" is a primary theme in
Hofmannsthal's *Elektra.*[12]

It was in 1906 when Richard Strauss, having initially declined to

---

[8] Quoted in Gilliam, 22.
[9] Gilliam, 22.
[10] Robert Marx, "Act Two," *Opera News* 63, no. 9 (March 1999): 19.
[11] Quoted in Marx, pp. 19–20.
[12] Gilliam, 22.

write a ballet on Hofmannsthal's *Der Triumph der Zeit*,[13] consented to set

Elektra (1903) to music. Although this was the beginning of a long

artistic relationship between the two men, this particular project did not

require much collaboration, since Strauss was the "major figure behind

Elektra's transformation from play to libretto."[14] Gilliam estimates that

Strauss reduced Hofmannsthal's text by nearly one third.[15] While these

intense cuts may have removed some of Hofmannsthal's psychological

complexities, they certainly reinforced the drama's focus on gesture or

action. In fact, one of the critical arguments with which Hofmannsthal

convinced Strauss to set *Elektra,* despite its apparent similarity to

Salome, was the intense burst of dramatic action which consumes the last

third of the drama:

> What is more, the rapid rising sequence of events . . . which
> leads up to victory and purification—a sequence which I can
> imagine much more powerful in music than in the written
> word—is not matched by anything of a corresponding, or even
> faintly similar kind in *Salome.*[16]

Here, Hofmannsthal highlighted the "rapid rising sequence of events" as

a key element of the work and alluded to the power of music to convey

this gesture better than words alone. All that Strauss did to telescope the

---

[13] *The Correspondence between Richard Strauss and Hugo von Hofmannsthal,*
trans. Hanns Hammelmann and Ewald Osers (London: William Collins Sons & Co. Ltd.,
1961), 1.

[14] Gilliam, 18.

[15] Gilliam, 36.

[16] *The Correspondence between Richard Strauss and Hugo von Hofmannsthal,* 4.

drama for the operatic stage seems to support the overall nature of Hofmannsthal's drama.

Although Hofmannsthal did not participate in the task of reducing his play to a manageable opera libretto, Strauss did ask Hofmannsthal to provide additional text in several cases. In a letter of 1908, Strauss wrote in regard to the opera's finale:

> Enclosed herewith your final verses which I am asking you to extend as much as possible. . . . Nothing new, just the same contents, repeated and working towards a climax.[17]

Although there is no doubt that the purpose of Strauss's request is to satisfy his overall musical plan, it seems to negate his previous efforts to reduce the text to its most necessary elements. Furthermore, by asking for more of the same words, Strauss's artistic goal seems to contradict Hofmannsthal's celebration of gesture above word.

One scene that may serve as another example of this aesthetic conflict between the two artists is the scene of recognition between Elektra and her brother, Orestes. Elektra's father, Agamemnon, was betrayed and murdered by Elektra's mother, Klytämnestra, and her paramour, Aegistheus. Elektra cannot forgive her mother and lives to avenge her father's murder. After Elektra fails to persuade her sister, Chrysothemis, to help her, Elektra is left alone. A stranger enters, and soon Elektra discovers it is her brother, Orestes, whom she believed to

---

[17] *The Correspondence between Richard Strauss and Hugo von Hofmannsthal*, 18.

be dead. It is at this moment in the drama that Elektra realizes her destiny; in Orestes she has found someone to carry out the *deed* of revenge.

In a letter of June 22, 1908, Strauss remarked:

> . . . I need a great moment of repose after Elektra's first shout: 'Orest!' I shall fit in a delicately vibrant orchestral interlude while Elektra gazes upon Orestes, now safely restored to her. I can make her repeat the stammered words: 'Orest, Orest, Orest!' several times. . . . Couldn't you insert here a few beautiful verses until I switch over to the sombre mood . . . ?[18]

Though Hofmannsthal reworked his verses to fit into the tender mood while Elektra gazes upon Orestes, the real concession here comes in the addition of a long orchestral interlude followed by a lyrical, closed aria for Elektra. In the following example from the libretto, note the indication of Strauss's musical insertion and the places where Strauss repeated Elektra's cry of "Orest!" In Hofmannsthal's original text, she calls out the name only once, at the beginning of the passage.

> Elektra[19]
> Orest!
> [Strauss's "delicately vibrant orchestral interlude"]
> Orest! Orest! Orest! Es rührt sich niemand! O lass deine
> Augen mich sehen, Traumbild, mir geschenktes Traumbild,
> schöner als alle Träume! Hehres, unbegreifliches, erhabenes
> Gesicht, o bleib' bei mir! Lös' nicht in Luft dich auf, vergeh'
> mir nicht, vergeh' mir nicht, es sei denn, dass ich jetzt gleich

[18] *The Correspondence between Richard Strauss and Hugo von Hofmannsthal,* 16.
[19] Hugo von Hofmannsthal, *Elektra,* libretto included with sound recording, trans. Boosey & Hawkes, Inc. (London OSA1269, 1966–1967), 20.

sterben muss und du dich anzeigst und mich holen kommst:
dann sterbe ich seliger, als ich gelebt! Orest! Orest! Orest!

<u>Elektra</u>
Orestes!
[Strauss's "delicately vibrant orchestral interlude"]
Orestes! Orestes! Orestes! No one is stirring! Oh let your eyes
gaze at me, dream-phantom, a vision which has been granted
me, fairer than any dream! Sublime, ineffable, noble
countenance, oh stay with me, do not melt into air, do not
vanish from my sight. Even if now I have to die, and you have
revealed yourself to me and come to fetch me, then I will die
happier than I have lived! Orestes! Orestes! Orestes!

It would be an error to imply that this musical extension in the form of
an aria has no precedent or context at all within the opera. It is, in fact, based
on the music we hear in Elektra's opening monologue, when she tenderly
laments the loss of her father. These following measures in A-flat major,
taken from that monologue, show Elektra's "longing for her father's love."[20]

Example 1, from Elektra's monologue, six bars before rehearsal 46[21]

---

[20] Paul Bekker, "*Elektra:* A Study by Paul Bekker," trans. Susan Gillespie, in
Richard Strauss and His World, ed. Bryan Gilliam (Princeton, NJ: Princeton University
Press, 1992), 384.
[21] Richard Strauss, *Elektra,* piano/vocal score (London: Boosey & Hawkes, 1943), 25.

It is this motive of longing that is re-awakened when Elektra recognizes Orestes, and it forms the basis of her fifty-four measure aria. The aria, which recalls the A-flat tonality of the longing in her monologue, ends with the following bars that echo Elektra's previous lamentations:

Example 2, from Elektra's aria, rehearsal 154a [22]

In some senses, it is almost is if time stops for a moment while Elektra absorbs into her being the reality that her innermost desires for revenge may be fulfilled. While this might seem a likely moment of repose in another drama, it undermines the "rapid rising sequence of events" that Hofmannsthal found integral to the nature of his drama. Some contemporary critics were quick to praise Strauss's musical choice here. Recently, Lawrence Gilman wrote of the recognition scene:

[22] Strauss, *Elektra*, 187.

> . . . Here we have once more the deeper and finer Strauss, the
> supremely moving tone-poet who portrayed the homecoming
> and death of Don Quixote, who gave us the tranquil close of
> "Ein Heldenleben." This scene is the musical apogee of the
> work. It has a richness of emotion, a depth of sorrowful
> tenderness, which set it among the noblest things in music.[23]

Paul Bekker, however, believed the result of the extension was a very noticeable attempt by Strauss to leave the audience with something musical to remember.

> The fact that passages of this kind make the strongest
> impression on the public cannot mislead more serious observers
> as to their lack of originality. I have no hesitation in judging the
> much-lauded A-flat-major passage—for many listeners the
> single refreshing moment of the evening—to be one of the
> weaker parts of the work. I do not even believe in the artistic-
> aesthetic necessity of this last-minute insertion. . . . May
> Strauss not have felt—consciously or unconsciously—a secret
> wish to offer something to those listeners who were inclined to
> indulge their ears?[24]

Even Lawrence Gilman admitted that aside from the musical success of the recognition scene, there are many passages "which are far from memorable—passages in which . . . the music declines from power and vitality into lamentable emptiness and commonness."[25]

---

[23] Lawrence Gilman, "Strauss and the Greeks," in *Nature in Music and Other Studies in Tone-Poetry of Today* (Freeport, NY: Books for Libraries Press, Inc., 1966), 129–130.

[24] Bekker, 399–400.

[25] Gilman, 130.

The real argument against what some praised as Strauss's musical greatness is that the end result suspends the dramatic action for too long. Perhaps this was Strauss's narcissistic attempt to leave the audience with a memorable "musical" moment. This flash of a self-serving aesthetic would definitely conflict with the thrust of Hofmannsthal's original text. Paul Bekker remarked:

> I almost wish that Hofmannsthal had not agreed to this alteration. The score of *Elektra* would be deprived of one of its most sure-fire effects, but its unity would not have been interrupted by this lyrical flourish.[26]

The fact that in later collaboration Strauss always deferred to Hofmannsthal's choice of subject is a great tribute to the librettist: in a way it almost reestablished a "pre-eminence of the libretto which was all but completely gone since Metastasio."[27] However, in the case of *Elektra*, it seems as if Strauss either could not or would not operate on the same aesthetic principles as his esteemed librettist. In this case of the recognition scene, one sees the *words* of Strauss's music superseding the *deed* of Hofmannsthal's drama.

---

[26] Bekker, 400.
[27] Patrick J. Smith, *The Tenth Muse: A Historical Study of the Opera Libretto* (New York: Schirmer Books, 1970), 364.

Bibliography

Bekker, Paul. "*Elektra:* A Study by Paul Bekker," trans. Susan Gillespie. In *Richard Strauss and His World,* ed. Bryan Gilliam, 372–405. Princeton, NJ: Princeton University Press, 1992.

The Correspondence between Richard Strauss and Hugo von Hofmannsthal, trans. Hanns Hammelmann and Ewald Osers. London: William Collins Sons & Co. Ltd., 1961.

Gilliam, Bryan. *Richard Strauss's Elektra.* Oxford: Clarendon Press, 1991.

Gilman, Lawrence. "Strauss and the Greeks." In *Nature in Music and Other Studies in Tone-Poetry of Today,* 111–132. Freeport, NY: Books for Libraries Press, Inc., 1966.

Hofmannsthal, Hugo von. *Elektra.* Libretto included with sound recording, trans. Boosey & Hawkes, Inc. London OSA1269, 1966–1967.

Kramer, Lawrence. "*Fin-de-siècle* Fantasies: *Elektra,* Degeneration and Sexual Science." *Cambridge Opera Journal* 5, no. 2 (July 1993): 141–165.

Mann, William. *Richard Strauss: A Critical Study of the Operas.* New York: Oxford University Press, 1966.

Marek, George R. "Cry of Anguish." *Opera News* 49 (December 8, 1984): 16–18.

Marx, Robert. "Act Two." *Opera News* 63, no. 9 (March 1999): 18–21.

Opel, Adolf. "The Legacies of Dissolution." Introduction to *The Sacred Spring: The Arts in Vienna 1898–1918,* by Nicolas Powell. London: Studio Vista, 1974.

Puffett, Derrick, ed. *Richard Strauss: Elektra.* Cambridge Opera Handbooks. Cambridge: Cambridge University Press, 1989.

Schorske, Carl E. *Fin-de-Siècle Vienna: Politics and Culture.* New York: Vintage Books, 1981.

Simon, John. "Daughter of Death." *Opera News* 56, no. 15 (April 11, 1992): 14–16, 18.

Smith, Patrick J. *The Tenth Muse: A Historical Study of the Opera Libretto.* New York: Schirmer Books, 1970.

Strauss, Richard. *Elektra,* Op. 58. London: Boosey & Hawkes, 1996.

Index

A

affect and *effect*, 137

agreement

  pronoun and antecedent, 124–26

  subject and verb, 123

analysis, 9–13

  compositional process and, 10

  definition, 9

  examples, 13–20

  questions to pursue, 10–13

  twentieth-century systems, 6

  types, 9

Anglo-Saxon roots, 109

articles, 31

B

Bach, Cantata No. 80, *Ein' feste Burg ist unser Gott,* 14–16

Baker's Biographical Dictionary of Musicians, 8th ed., 26

bibliography, 25–26, 48–49, 66–78

  annotating, 49

  assembling, 25

  format, 66–78

    articles in collections, 73

    articles in dictionaries and encyclopedias, 70–72

    articles in periodicals, 72

    books, 66–70

    dissertations, 70

    electronic resources, 75–78

    interviews and correspondence, 75

    recordings, 74

    scores, 73

  published bibliographies, 26

  secondhand references, 49

  what to include, 49

biographies, 30

Brook, Barry S., *Thematic Catalogues in Music: An Annotated Bibliography,* 30

C

catalogs, 26

  on-line (*see* electronic resources)

challenges of writing about music, 2

Charles, Sydney Robinson, *A Handbook of Music and Music Literature in Sets and Series,* 32

Chicago Manual of Style, 14th ed., xiv–xv, 59, 60, Chapter 5 *passim,* 122, 138, 144

colon, 142

comma, 139–41

  appositives, 139

  compound and complex sentences, 140

  introductory phrases, 140

  restrictive and nonrestrictive phrases and clauses, 140

  series, 139

composer's intent, 12

concert report, 88–91

  how to proceed, 90

  purpose, 89

  research, 89

conclusion, 42, 120, 153

Crocker, Richard L., *A History of Musical Style*, 28
cultural studies and analysis, 7, 11

D
dangling participle, 129
dash, 143
databases on CD-ROM. *See* electronic resources
deconstruction and new criticism, 7
describing musical events, 147
diagrams and tables, 45
dictionaries, 133
discreet and *discrete*, 137
Dissertation Abstracts, 35
dissertations, 31
Doctoral Dissertation in Musicology On-Line, 36
draft, 43
    using a computer, 43
Duckles, Vincent H., and Ida Reed, *Music Reference and Research Materials: An Annotated Bibliography*, 5th ed., xiii, xiv, 21
due to and *because of*, 137

E
editing and revising, 50–54
    for coherence, 52
    for detail, 53
    grammar checker, 52
    process, 52–54
    reading aloud, 53
    spell-checker, 51
    using a computer, 50
electronic resources, 33–37
    databases on CD-ROM, 33
    Internet, 35
    link sites, 36
    on-line catalogs, 33
ellipsis, 64
endnotes. *See* footnotes
essay examinations, 97–101
    common errors, 99–101
    how to proceed, 98
    preparing for, 98
    purpose, 97
euphemism, 104
evaluating resources, 37

F
fewer and *less*, 138
footnotes, 46–50
    common knowledge, 47
    direct and indirect quotations, 46
    footnotes or endnotes, 48
    format, 66–78
        articles in collections, 73
        articles in dictionaries and encyclopedias, 70
        articles in periodicals, 72
        books, 66–70
        dissertations, 70
        electronic resources, 75–78
        interviews and correspondence, 75
        recordings, 74
        scores, 43
foreign-language sources, 38
foreign terms, 81, 109, 134
format
    for bibliography (*see* bibliography, format)
    for footnotes (*see* footnotes, format)
    for projects, 59–62
        font and size, 61
        justification, 61
        margins, 60
        page numbers, 62
        paper, 60
    for quotations (*see* quotation)

G
genre, form, style, 145–47
Gesualdo, "Moro, lasso," 13
Grout, Donald J., and Claude V. Palisca, *A History of Western Music*, 6th ed., 28

H
Harnack, Andres, and Eugene Klippinger, *Online / A Reference Guide to Using Internet Sources*, 76
Harvard Biographical Dictionary of Music, 26
Heyer, Anna, comp., *Historical Sets, Collected Editions, and Monuments of Music*, 3rd ed., 32
Hill, George R., and Norris L. Stephens, *Collected Editions, Historical Sets, and Monuments of Music*, 32

histories of music, 28–30
however, still, yet, hence, 141
hyphen, 143

I

I, 107
inappropriate writing about music, 3–7
  anachronistic analysis, 6
  biographical interpretation, 4
  fanciful comparisons, 3
  listing of events, 5
  programmatic interpretation, 4
  sentimental descriptions, 4
in-depth, 112
International Index to Music Periodicals
    (IIMP), 34
International Inventory of Music
    Literature (RILM), 30, 31, 35
Internet. *See* electronic resources
introduction, 41, 119, 153
its and *it's,* 136

J

journals. *See* articles
  on-line, 36

L

Latin roots, 109
lecture-recital, 101
Li, Xia, and Nancy B. Crane, *Electronic
    Styles: A Handbook for Citing
    Electronic Information,* 76
Library of Congress catalog numbers
  M2, 32
  M3, 32
  ML410, 30
link sites. *See* electronic resources
Liszt, *A Faust Symphony,* 18
literal sense of words, 110

M

metaphor, 131
  mixed, 131
MLA style, 59
modifiers
  placement of, 128–30
  reliance on, 113
Mozart, Concerto for Piano
    and Orchestra in C Minor,
    K. 491, 16

musical examples, 44, 153
  annotating, 45
  format, 82
Music and Society Series, 29
Music Index, 31
music lexicons, 26–28
  multivolume works, 27
  single-volume works, 26
musicological research, types of, 7
Musik in Geschichte und Gegenwart, Die,
    2nd ed., 27

N

names, medieval and Renaissance, 135
neologism, 110
*New Grove Dictionary of American
    Music,* 28
New Grove Dictionary of Jazz, 28
*New Grove Dictionary of Musical
    Instruments,* 28
*New Grove Dictionary of Music
    and Musicians,* 2nd ed., xi, 27
New Grove Dictionary of Opera, 28
New Harvard Dictionary of Music, 27
New Oxford History of Music, 29
Norton Introduction to Music History
    Series, 29
notes and keys, citing, 80
not un- construction, 113
noun strings, 112

O

only, 128
outline, 40–43
  revising, 42

P

paragraph, coherence of, 118
parallel construction, 116
parentheses, 144
passive voice, 15
period, 139
periods, historical, referring to, 78
plagiarism, 55–57
  consequences of, 56
  definition, 55
  detecting, 57
plural forms of Latin and Greek words,
    134
possessives, formation of, 133

Prentice Hall History of Music Series, 29
primary sources, 22
principal and *principle,* 138
printing, 54
program notes, 91–97
  audience, 91
  early music, 94
  familiar repertory, 96
  limits, 93
  new music, 95
  purpose, 91
  research, 92
  texts and translations, 96
pronouns
  case of, 126
  relative, 126–28
proofreading, 54
prose, kinds of, 104
punctuation, 138–144

Q
qualitative judgments, 148
quotation
  direct and indirect, 46
  editorial additions to, 64
  format, 62–64
    block quotations, 63
    short quotations, 63
quotation marks, placement of, 142

R
Radice, Mark A., *Irvine's Writing
    about Music,* 3rd ed., xiii, xiv
reception history. *See* musicological
    research
recordings, 32
redundant couplets, 112
research
  definition, 24
  ways to start, 25
  when to stop, 38
revising. *See* editing and revising
RILM. *See International Inventory
    of Music Literature*
Rosensteil, Leonie, general ed.,
    Schirmer History of Music, 28
run-on sentence, 123

S
scores, 32
secondary literature, 22

semicolon, 141
seminar presentation, 83–88
  handout, 86
  multimedia presentation, 87
  organization, 84–86
  recorded examples, 85
  research, 84
  time limits, 84
  tone, 88
sentence fragment, 122
sentence structure, 114–18
  variety of, 117
sharp, flat, natural. See notes and keys,
    citing
sic, 65
slang, 109
spelling, 132
split infinitive, 131
sports jargon, 105
stance of writer, 106
stock couplets, 113
Stolba, K. Marie, *The Development
    of Western Music: A History,*
    2nd ed., 28
Stravinsky, *The Rite of Spring,* 19
Strunk, William, and E. B. White,
    The Elements of Style, xiv, xv

T
technical terms, 105, 144
thematic catalogs, 30
thesis, 40, 153
titles of musical works, 78–80
  generic, 79
  italics or quotation marks, 79
  opus numbers, 80
  subtitles, 79
tone of writing, 105, 153
  slangy, 106
  stilted, 106
topic
  choosing, 21–23
  developing topics from musical
    works, 13–20
  kinds, 23
  proper scope, 22
  and thesis (*see* thesis)
transitions, 120
Troyka, Lynn Quitman, *Simon &
    Schuster Handbook for Writers,*
    5th ed., xiv, xv, 122, 138, 144

Turabian, Kate L., *A Manual for Writers of Term Papers, Theses, and Dissertations*, 5th ed., revised and expanded by Bonnie Birtwhistle Honigsblum, xiv, 59, Chapter 5 *passim*, 144

U
URL (Uniform Resource Locator), 75, 77

V
verbing, 111
Verdi, *Otello*, 17
Verzeichnis. *See* thematic catalogs

W
whose and *who's*, 137
Wingell, Richard, and Silvia Herzog, *Introduction to Research in Music*, xi, xiv, 21, 65
word choice, 108–11
   variety of, 111
word order, 115
writing
   improving, 102, 103
   kinds of, 103

Y
your and *you're*, 136